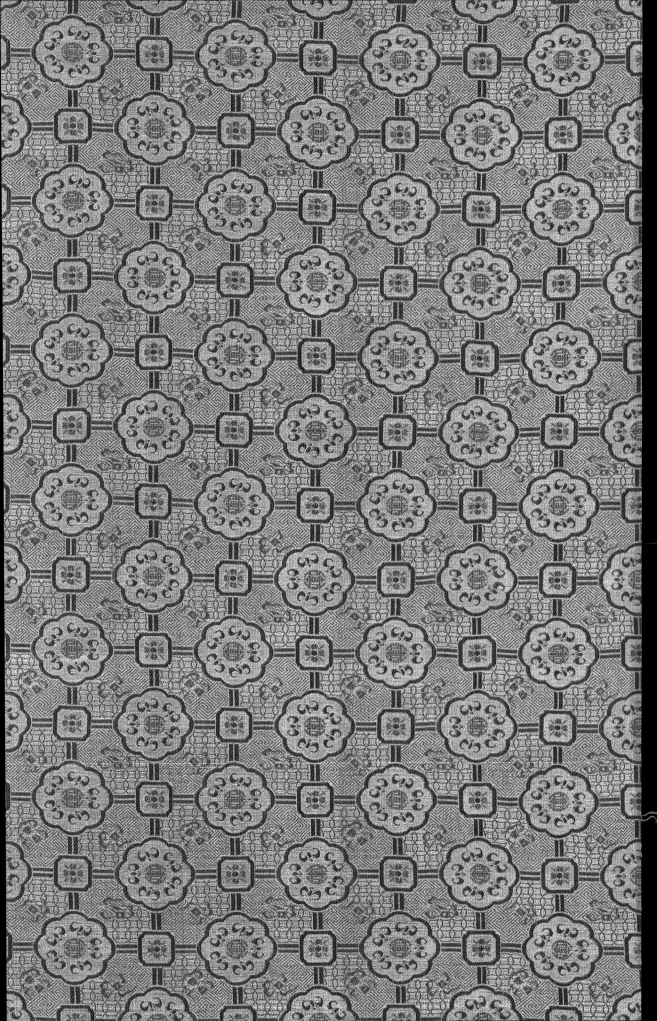

HUA SONG
Stories of The Chinese Diaspora

Christine Suchen Lim

LONG RIVER PRESS

SAN FRANCISCO

Hua Song 《华颂》 means 'in praise of the Chinese community'.

The Singapore Tourism Board
and the Hua Song Project Consultants

Team SNP

Publisher	Shirley Hew
Publishing Manager	Shova Loh
Editors	Tan Mike Tze
	Candice Chan
	Jia Zhengqing
Creative Director	Tuck Loong
Graphic Designer	Winson Chua
Marketing & Operations Manager	Clara Wong

The publishers wish to thank for their assistance and generosity:
Ng Chin Keong and Chang Yueh Siang of the Chinese Heritage Centre, Singapore
Goh Eck Kheng, Tan Lai Huat and Lee Sing Tiong

Artefact Photography	Yu Hui Ying and Lek Hui Hui
Archival Images and Copyrights	Lim Bee Leng and G Uma Devi

Published by special arrangement with
SNP International Publishing Pte Ltd
A subsidiary of SNP Corporation Ltd
1 Kim Seng Promenade, #18-01 Great World City, East Tower
Singapore 237994
Tel: (65) 6826 9600, Fax: (65) 6820 3341
Email: snpinternational@snpcorp.com, Website: www.snpcorp.com

Long River Press
360 Swift Ave., Suite #48
South San Francisco, CA 94080, USA
www.longriverpress.com

Printed in Singapore
ISBN 1 59265 043 0

Library of Congress Cataloging-in-Publication Data

Lim, Su-chen Christine.
Hua Song: Stories of The Chinese Diaspora / Christine Suchen Lim. p. cm.
ISBN: 1-59265-043-0 (pbk.)

1. Chinese – Foreign countries I. Title. II. Title: Stories of The Chinese Diaspora
DS732.L53 2005
909'.04951 – dc22   2004031110

Shoemaker with native Indonesian, c. 1867

Family portrait, America, c. 1935

contents

Chinatown in New York, c. 1939–1945

foreword

The history of Chinese emigration really began when large numbers of labourers left the shores of China to work in foreign lands during the nineteenth century. For a thousand years before that, though there had been traders, political exiles, deserters, criminals and seamen who left and did not return, there were not many of these at any one time. The number of Chinese sojourners only began to rise significantly, especially in Southeast Asia, after the arrival of the Europeans in the sixteenth century.

The truly dramatic change came after the Industrial Revolution in Europe and the end of slavery in Africa, when the need to harvest raw materials from the mines and plantations of Southeast Asia and South America led the West to import Chinese and Indian labourers to their colonies. During this same period, gold was found in parts of North America and Australasia, and this drew the Chinese eastward and southward across the Pacific Ocean. By the end of the century, the call of Nanyang ('Southern Ocean') and Jinshan ('Gold Mountain') had tempted hundreds of thousands to leave their homes in Fujian and Guangdong. When these men and women returned with new wealth, ideas and skills, the towns and cities in South China were greatly transformed.

The more we learn about Chinese migrants, the more we realise how different their experiences were. They were normally divided between those who looked to China and those who settled down and wished to identify with their adopted country. Their outlooks were contingent upon where they went and how ready they were to live among non-Chinese. Where they lived as large communities, as in many cities in Southeast Asia, they were slow to understand

indigenous values and were often made to feel unwelcome. Elsewhere, in the migrant societies of North America and Australasia, the Chinese were systematically discriminated against for nearly a hundred years. Yet, in recent times, many Chinese have found local cultures increasingly congenial and have even learnt to admire the new values that they represent.

The story of how these Chinese set forth, how they were treated where they landed, how some returned and others fought to stay on, and how their descendants helped to develop their adopted lands, is succinctly and graphically told in this volume by Suchen Christine Lim. With her excellent choice of quotes and extracts, she captures the story of the Chinese as a global presence and makes their words sing out to us.

Migration is now a more global story than at any time in history. The Chinese experience today may no longer be distinctive. What still makes their story remarkable is the role that Chinese miners, plantation workers and entrepreneurs played in the economic development of Southeast Asia and the Americas, and especially their contributions towards opening up the goldfields of North America and Australasia. *Hua Song* highlights this history most effectively. The descendants of those Chinese, their compatriots and all who are interested in the history of migration will find this book a splendid reminder of that unique past.

Professor Wang Gungwu
Director, East Asian Institute

序言

华人移民历史19世纪时真正开始。当时，来自中国沿海地区的华工成批涌到海外工作。之前的一千年内，已有少量商人、政治流亡者、逃兵、犯人和海员外出中国，久居不返。随着16世纪欧洲人的来临，这小规模的迁移活动才有增加的趋势，尤其是在东南亚一带。

欧洲工业革命以及非洲奴隶制度的结束，是华人迁移海外历程的转捩点。欧洲人急需人力开发东南亚和南美洲的矿场与种植园，因此从中国和印度运来了大批劳工，应付需求。与此同时，在北美洲和澳亚洲各部分相继发现了金矿，吸引了华人跨越太平洋淘金。到了19世纪末，已有数十万中国人远离福建和广东的家乡，回应了'南洋'和'金山'的呼唤。这些男女游子带着他们的新财富、概念与技能返回，大大革新了中国南部市镇与城市的面貌。

我们对华人移民越了解，就越会发现他们经历的遭遇不同。他们基本上可分为倾向中国的，和欲归属所居住国，渴望在那儿定居的。他们的思想随着居住地而改变，决定于他们是否做好心理准备与非华人共处一处。凡是华人组织大社群共同聚居的地方，如东南亚的数个镇城，他们对当地价值观的了解就会十分缓慢，常使得他们不受欢迎。在其他地方，即北美洲和澳亚洲的移民社会，华人面对了将近一整个世纪的歧视。尽管如此，许多华人近期内也越来越觉得当地文化也有悦心之处，甚至还学会了欣赏这些文化所涵盖着的新鲜价值观。

华人移民故事包括了他们迁移的起源、在所居处所受的待遇、有些人为何归返故乡、其他人怎么为留在异乡而奋斗、他们的后代如何在异乡落地生根，为该国发展作出贡献。本书作者林苏贞简练的文笔，绘声绘色地把这一切勾画、畅述出来。她以优质的语录和摘要，从环球角度捕捉海外华人的故事，使得主角们的心声仿佛在我们心中娓娓环绕。

比起历史的任何时代，如今的人口迁移现象最为全球化。华人的经历现在可能不再特殊。海外华人的故事之所以还会让人绕梁三日、荡气回肠，是华人矿工、种植园工和华商如何在东南亚与美洲为当地经济发展作出巨大贡献。尤其是他们开拓北美洲和澳亚洲金矿的事迹，功不可抹。《华颂》非常有效地突出了这历史。那些华人的子孙、同伴和所有对移民历史有兴趣的人，都会把这本书视为那独特过往最好的提醒。

王赓武教授
所长，东亚研究所

Studio portrait, Singapore, late 1800s/early 1900s

prologue

Since the earliest times, Chinese merchants had
ventured beyond China's shores to the South Seas and
beyond. This trickle of migration became a tide in the
nineteenth century when war and the collapse of the
agrarian economy in southern China led to catastrophic
social conditions that drove thousands to distant lands
in search of a livelihood. Coolies were packed like pigs
to the slaughter and shipped around the world.

The story of these migrant workers and sojourners
is that of our great-grandfathers and uncles, and our
great-grandmothers and aunts. Their tale of suffering,
fortitude and enterprise is part of the continuing story
of the Chinese overseas.

You are invited to take a thread and join in the
weaving of this story of ordinary men and women with
extraordinary courage and resilience.

开场白

从最早时候，华商们就出征南海。这种小型的移民活动在20世纪形
成了浪潮。那时，国内的战争和传染病迫使成千上万的人到海外谋
生。苦力们像被送到屠宰场的猪只，成批地被塞进船里，送到世界
各个角落。

这些流离海外的劳动者的故事，是我们曾祖父、曾叔公、曾祖母、
曾姑婆的故事。他们流离、受苦、坚忍和进取的故事，是至今还未
完结的海外华人的故事中的一部分。

请拿起你们手中的线，一同编织这些有着超凡勇气和韧性的平凡男
女的故事。

Gold

During the nineteenth century, news of gold discoveries in America, Australia, New Zealand and South Africa drew thousands of Chinese to these distant shores. Stories of gold nuggets being picked up from the ground entered the dreams of young men hungry for work and a way to support their families. Later, the demand for labour to build railways in America and Canada brought thousands more while other sojourners went to Southeast Asia, to the tin mines of Malaya, and to Indonesia, Vietnam and the Philippines.

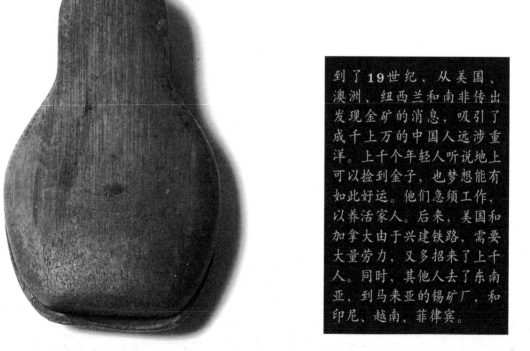

到了19世纪，从美国、澳洲、纽西兰和南非传出发现金矿的消息，吸引了成千上万的中国人远涉重洋。上千个年轻人听说地上可以捡到金子，也梦想能有如此好运。他们急须工作，以养活家人。后来，美国和加拿大由于兴建铁路，需要大量劳力，又多招来了上千人。同时，其他人去了东南亚，到马来亚的锡矿厂，和印尼、越南、菲律宾。

China, late 1800s/early 1900s

曾祖父说："在金
山，一个一顿吃的
肉，足以给一家人
吃上一个月。是，
很多很多的肉。
一家人越饿，故事
就讲得越夸张，肉
块和金块也就显得
越真实。

汤婷婷，*China Men*

Streets of Shanghai, late 1800s/early 1900s

'On the Gold Mountain, a man eats enough meat at one eat to feed a family for a month', said Great Grandfather. 'Yes, slabs of meat'. The hungrier the family got, the bigger the stories, the more real the meat and the gold.

Maxine Hong Kingston, *China Men*

The coastal city of Hangzhou, late 1800s/early 1900s

gold mountain dream

Dislocated by war and banditry, impoverished by drought and famine, cajoled by recruiting agents with the promise of high wages and lured by dreams of gold, hundreds of thousands of filial sons, good husbands and fathers, uprooted ourselves and left our homes.

Landless and starving, with only hope for the future, we sailed from the ports of Xiamen, Guangzhou, Fuzhou, Hong Kong, Ningbo and Shanghai from the 1850s to the 1930s, for places as far away as:

- Indonesia
- Malaysia
- The Philippines
- Singapore
- Thailand
- Vietnam
- Canada
- South America
- America
- Australia
- New Zealand
- The South Pacific
- Britain
- France
- Russia
- India
- South Africa

Our hopes were high. We had dreams of finding wealth and happiness. May the Gods of Prosperity, Fortune and

金山梦

战乱与匪祸迫使我们离开家园；旱灾和饥荒使得我们一贫如洗；我们梦想着黄金，梦想着发财。数以万计饿着肚子的孝顺儿子、妻子的好丈夫、儿女的好父亲们，由于相信了劳工代办们高薪承诺的甜言蜜语，又或是遭到不良代办的绑架，离开了故乡。从1850年代到1930年代，我们乘着船从厦门、广州、福州、香港、宁波和上海出发，驶向遥远的彼岸，如：

- 印尼
- 马来西亚
- 菲律宾
- 新加坡
- 泰国
- 越南

- 加拿大
- 南美洲
- 美国
- 澳洲
- 纽西兰
- 南太平洋

- 英国
- 法国
- 俄国
- 印度
- 南非

我们满怀希望。我们梦想着找到财富与幸福。愿福、禄、寿三星眷佑我们！

Arrival at Singapore, c. 1900

One drum,
   Two gongs,
All Hakkas,
   Listen to my song.
No harm listening to my persuasive song.
   It is good to take one's own path.

Do not mind if the journey is long,
   Nor fear the hassle.

North, south, east, west,
   You can travel in all directions.
All places in the world are your domains.
   Be it prefecture, country or province,
      You can live in the city or the town.

Ever heard of foreigners coming to China?
   Chinese people going overseas,
Tens of thousands in Gold Mountain,
   Ten thousand in India.

Hakka Drum Song

一打鼓，
二打锣，
众客民，
听我歌：
我歌劝散听无讹，
各人走散各人好，

莫嫌路远怕奔波。

东南西北任汝所至，
普天之下皆王土，
或州或县或省府，
市镇通衢皆可处。

更闻人自外国来，
中国人多海外往，
数十万人在金山，
数万人在印度。

《劝散歌》

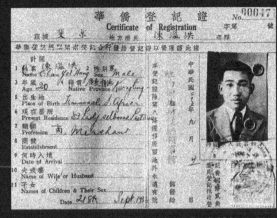

Certificate of registration, Johannesburg, South Africa, c. 1910

Members of the Chinese Labour Corps, France, c. 1917

Coming ashore at Honolulu, late 1800s/early 1900s

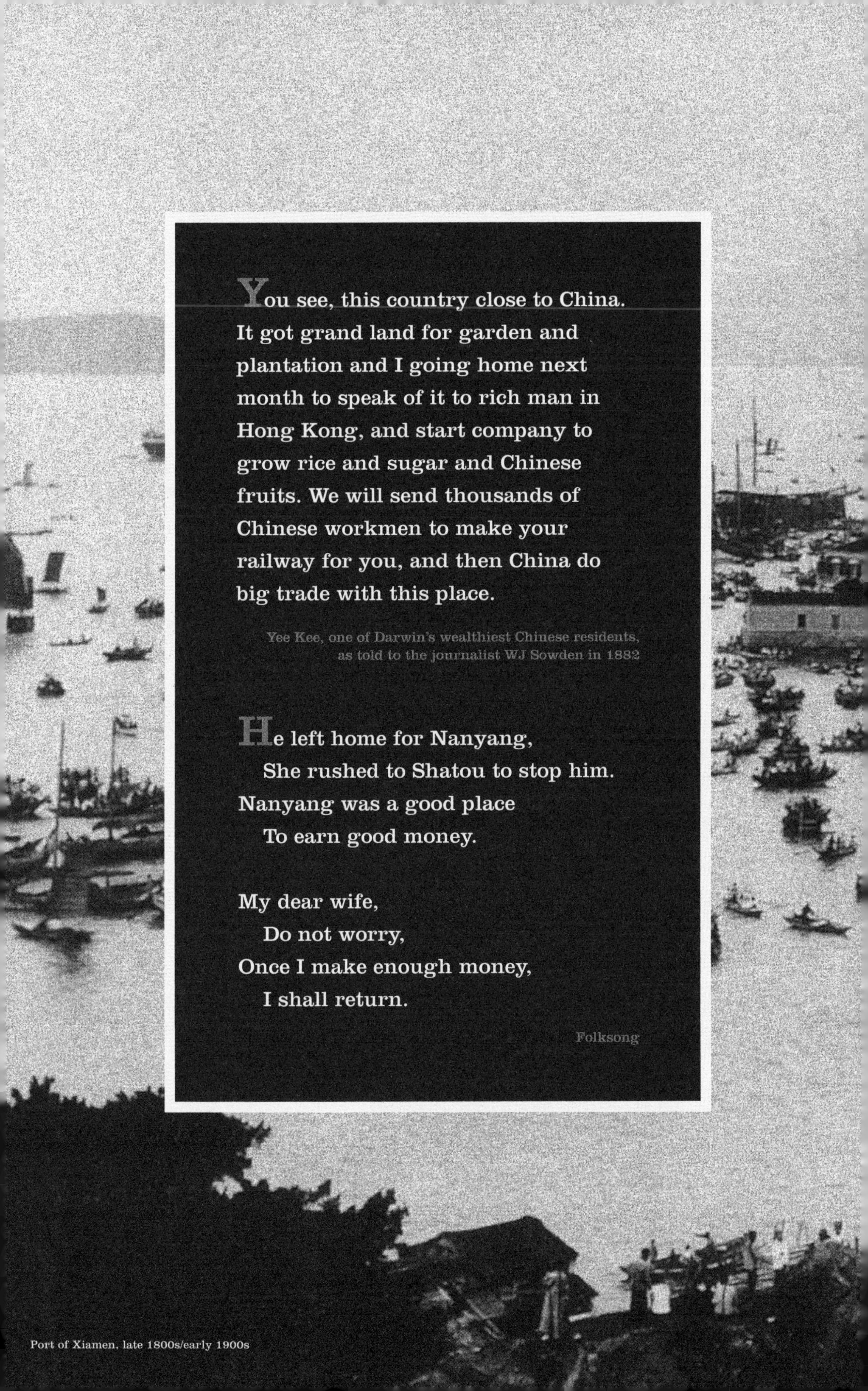

You see, this country close to China. It got grand land for garden and plantation and I going home next month to speak of it to rich man in Hong Kong, and start company to grow rice and sugar and Chinese fruits. We will send thousands of Chinese workmen to make your railway for you, and then China do big trade with this place.

Yee Kee, one of Darwin's wealthiest Chinese residents, as told to the journalist WJ Sowden in 1882

He left home for Nanyang,
    She rushed to Shatou to stop him.
Nanyang was a good place
    To earn good money.

My dear wife,
    Do not worry,
Once I make enough money,
    I shall return.

Folksong

Port of Xiamen, late 1800s/early 1900s

你看，这国家靠近中
国。它有大片可用来
耕种的土地；我下个
月就回家和香港的有
钱人谈，看能不能在
这里开公司生产米、
糖和中国水果。我们
会找上千个中国人替
你建铁路，中国就可
以跟这里做大生意。

又名、达尔文最富有的居民之一，
1882年与记者 WJ Sowden 交谈

阿哥出门去过番，
妹子赶到汕头揽，
番邦赚钱番邦使，

贤妻唔使多挂虑，
赚到银纸转唐山。

民谣

the risks

Dreams of finding freedom and wealth in other parts of the world had enticed the Chinese to leave their homeland as early as the Ming Dynasty.

The law in China is far too severe and inhibitive. It is almost impossible to do anything without offending the law at all. Why don't we go overseas to enjoy the vast freedom?

Wang Zhi, a prominent merchant of the Ming Dynasty, *Discussion of Piracy, Vol. I*

Chinese sailors coming to the country [Cambodia] note with pleasure that it is not necessary to wear clothes, and since rice is easily had, women easily persuaded, houses easily run, furniture easily come by, and trade easily carried on, a great many sailors desert to take up permanent residence.

China, late 1800s/early 1900s

In the early days, the dangers of leaving our homeland were horrendous. During the early Qing period, the law prohibited the Chinese from doing so, and those who left for the South Seas were beheaded when caught.

Ta Ch'ing Lu Li: Fundamental Laws Concerning Emigration

All officers of government, soldiers, and private citizens, who clandestinely proceed to sea to trade, or who remove to foreign islands for the purpose of inhabiting and cultivating the same, shall be punished according to the law against communicating with rebels and enemies, and consequently suffer death by being beheaded.

Sir George Thomas Staunton (trans.),

冒险

早自明朝，许多中国人为了追求在海外找到自由与财富的梦想，离开了自己的故乡。

国中法制森严，动辄触禁，孰与海外逍遥哉?

王直，明朝著名海商，《海寇议前》

唐人之为水手者
利其国中不着衣裳
且米粮易求
妇女易得
屋室易辨
器用易足
买卖易为
往往皆逃逸於彼

周达观，《真腊风土记》，1296年

早先时候，我们离开故乡得冒很大的风险。清朝初期，朝廷明令禁止人民出境。前往南海的人，一旦被捉到就被斩首。

无论官员、兵士或平民，只要非法参与海上贸易，或是搬至海外岛屿居住和从事生产活动，将以叛国通敌罪论处，处以斩首之刑。

Sir George Thomas Staunton (trans.),

The Fundamental Laws and a Selection from the

Supplementary Statutes of the Penal Code of China

Sailors sealing the hold, c. 1860

big wind, big storm

In 1893, the prohibition against overseas travel was lifted by imperial decree. However, even before this, thousands of brave hearts had already left the country from the ports of southern China. We were fleeing our war-torn and impoverished land so that we could work and send money home to our families. We boarded coolie ships, filled with hope and trepidation.

A Chinese merchant in Australia, for instance, wants 800 coolies for gold diggings; he sends an order to his merchant-friend in Hong Kong, who procures the coolies, charters the steamer, and despatches her with the people.

HA Firth, emigration officer for British Guinea at Calcutta, 1875

The voyage by sea to unknown and distant lands such as Malaya, Australia, North America and South Africa was often fraught with danger. Conditions on board the ships were appalling. Once we left the ports, we were at the mercy of the crew.

…when quitting Macau, we proceeded to sea, we were confined to the hold below; some were even shut up in bamboo cages, or chained to iron posts, and a few were indiscriminately selected and flogged as a means of intimidating all others; while we cannot estimate the deaths that, in all, took place, from sickness, blows, hunger, thirst, or from suicide by leaping into the sea.

The Cuban Commission Report: The Hidden History of the Chinese in Cuba, 1876

The rate of passage-money when paid in advance is about $7 to $8… the rate of passage on credit being about $12… Immigrants who owe for their passages are detained on board, the *kay tows* [headmen] being allowed to land and find employers for their bands who will settle for their passage-money. If there is demand for coolies, the *kay tow* makes a profit, getting perhaps $20 per head for his band, whereas they will probably have cost him $13 to $14. The usual price paid by the employer is from $17 to $20, the margin between this and the passage rate constitutes his profit.

Report on the Condition of Chinese Labourers in the Colony,
Straits Settlements Legislative Council, 1876

On the ninth of the third moon we boarded our sailing ship. There were over 100 passengers from Punyu, several tens from Hungshan, over 100 from the Four Districts, and several tens of Hakkas from Kowloon—330 altogether. The interpreter was a Hungshan man. After leaving Hong Kong we had two months of fine weather and smooth seas. But when rabbits and dogs live together, it is hard to make a flock of them. There were a great many quarrels. Sometimes the pigs fought with the horses and the horses would kick the pigs.

In the third month there were strong winds and high seas. It was impossible to cook food... In the holds where our beds were, there was a foot of water. Then all the passengers began crying out, 'save us!' I did not hear on whom they were calling to save them. A Four District boy, 12 years old, and myself were the only ones who did not call out. One man belonging to our village rolled up his bedding and fled, but I don't know where he intended to go. We were all preserved in safety with the exception of a Hungshan man who died at sea and was buried when we reached port.

James Shum, former gold miner,
on his voyage to New Zealand

Coolies aboard ship, c. 1900

大风大浪

到了1893年，朝廷降旨取消出海禁令。可是，在禁令被取消之前，无畏的我们已经成千上万地从南边的各个港口离开中国。我们逃离了这片因战火而荒芜的土地，为的是能赚钱寄回家乡养家糊口。我们满怀着希望、彷徨，登上了船。

> 例如，一个澳洲华商需要800名苦力为他淘金；他把定单寄给在香港的商人朋友。这朋友就会招雇苦力，租一艘船，把这些苦力送达澳洲。
>
> HA Firth, 1875年

前往马来亚、澳洲、加利福尼亚和南非如此遥远的陌生之地的航程常危机重重。船上的各条件差得惊人。我们一离开了港口，就任船员摆布。

> ...离开了澳门，到了海上，我们就被关在舱底；有些人甚至被关进竹笼里或被绑在铁柱上。一些人被随意挑出来鞭打，只为了杀鸡儆猴，吓吓其他人；船上病死、遭毒打而死、饿死、渴死或投海自尽的人，不计其数。
>
> The Cuban Commission Report: The Hidden History of the Chinese in Cuba, 1876年

> 如果预先缴付，船费大概是7至8元...如果赊欠的话，船费大概是12元...赊欠船费的乘客都被扣在船上，只有头家（带苦力来的人）可以下船，为苦力找雇主，为他们缴付船费。如果有雇主，头家就从中获利：他按每人20元向雇主收钱，但他花在苦力身上的钱每人才13至14元。通常雇主们只愿付每人17到20元不等，扣除船费后，剩下的就是头家的利润。
>
> Report on the Condition of Chinese Labourers in the Colony Straits Settlements Legislative Council, 1876年

> 我们三月初九上了船。船上的乘客中，百多人来自盘屿，几十人来自红山，百多人来自四区，还有来自九龙的几十个客家人－总共330个人。翻译员是个红山人。离开香港的头两个月，天气晴朗、风平浪静。可是，当兔子与狗儿一起生活时，要让它们和睦相处是件难事。船上发生了许多争执。有时候，猪仔会和马儿打架，而马儿也会踢猪仔。第三个月，海上出现了强风骇浪。不可能煮东西吃。我们的床垫都在船底，而船底积了一尺的水。然后，乘客们都开始大叫：'救救我们啊！' 我没听到他们在呼唤谁来救他们。唯有一个十二岁的四区小男孩和我自己没有喊叫。有一个和我们同乡的男子把床垫卷了起来打算逃跑，但我不知道他打算逃到哪里去。我们都活下来了，除了一个红山人。他在途中死了，我们到了港口才把他埋葬。
>
> James Shum, 前金矿矿工，描述到纽西兰的海程

Arrival at Angel Island, San Francisco, c. 1920

Letter of domicile,
Cuba, c. 1860

arrival in the new land

**When the coolie ships arrived at ports like San Francisco
and Singapore, we were met by agents, usually men who
spoke our dialect. We were then herded into wagons. New
arrival Huie Kin recalled the day he first saw America.**

On a clear crisp morning in 1868, on the seventh year of our Emperor
T'ung Chih, the mists lifted and we sighted land for the first time since
we left the shores of Kwangtung over 60 days before. To be actually at
the Golden Gate of the land of our dreams! The feeling that welled up in
us was indescribable... We rolled up our bedding, packed our baskets,
straightened our clothes and waited. In those days there were no
immigration laws or tedious examinations; people came and went freely.
Somebody brought to the pier large wagons for us. Out of the general
babble, someone called out in our local dialect, and, like sheep recognizing
the voice only, we blindly followed, and soon were piling into one of the
waiting wagons. Everything was so strange and so exciting that my
memory of the landing is just a big blur...

Dorothy and Thomas Hoobler, *The Chinese American Family Album*

**While we looked upon our arrival in the new land with great
hope, others saw us differently. Some were curious, others
hostile. Sometimes boys threw stones at us.**

A living stream of the blue-coated men of Asia, bending long bamboo poles
across their shoulders, from which depend packages of bedding, matting,
clothing, and things we know neither the names or the uses, pours down
the plank the moment the word is given, 'All ready!' They appear to be of
an average age of 25 years—very few being under 15, and none apparently
over 40 years—and though somewhat less in stature than Caucasians,
healthy, active and able-bodied to a man...

They are all dressed in coarse but clean and new cotton blouses and loose
baggy breeches, blue cotton stockings which reach to the knees, and
slippers or shoes with heavy wooden soles... For two mortal hours the
blue stream pours down from the steamer upon the wharf; a regiment has
landed already, and they still come...

Albert S Evans, 'From the Orient Direct', *Atlantic Monthly*, 1869

Medical examination, China, late 1800s/early 1900s

William Head Quarantine Station, Vancouver Island, c. 1915

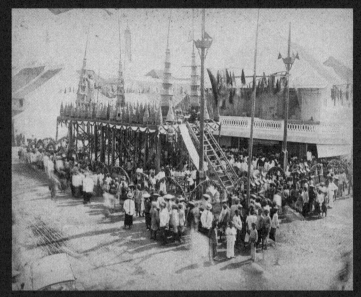

Port of Java, c. 1890

登陆新天地

当苦力乘船到达陌生港口，如旧金山，便会有代办接见我们。这些代办通常会讲我们的方言。我们跟着就被赶上马车。**Huie Kin**记得第一次见到美国的那天。

1868年，即同治七年，一个清凉的早晨，迷雾散去了。离开广东60多天，我们终于见到了第一片陆地，而且来到了梦境中的金门！胸头涌上的感觉真是无法形容。我们卷起床垫、收拾东西、整理衣服、等待着。那时没有移民法律，没有累人的关检；大家都来去自如。有人驾了大马车到码头载我们。一片喧闹之中，有人以我们家乡的方言喊我们，而我们像听声音的绵羊，盲目跟着，就这样上了马车。一切都如此陌生，

Saint John's Island Quarantine Station, Singapore, c. 1920

澳洲和纽西兰的报章批评我们。

他们20到200个人成一组，东西吊在竹竿上，竿子则扛在肩膀上。他们不走不跑，而是配合肩上担子的摇晃频率快步前进。他们松松的鞋子拍打着脚板，或拖在地上，发出沙沙的声音，不停为他们高而嘹亮的嗓子作合音。

Bathurst Free Press, 1858年5月26日和9月1日

我们在这片新天地里找到的不是黄金和幸福，而是迷惘、剥削、排斥和侮辱。我们被视为商品和货物，只能靠出卖力气和劳动来换取食宿。苦力们在西印度群岛像奴隶一样被剥削、售卖。

...我们被分成三个等级－一级、二级、三级－在市场上售卖；我们被迫脱下全身的衣服，以便让人查看我们的身体，议定买价。这是我们的耻辱。

The Cuban Commission Report: The Hidden History of the Chinese in Cuba 英文原文，1876年

在世界其他地区，苦力都是签了契约的外来劳工；他们以自己的体力干活来赚取金钱。

来这里的中国人很多，回去的却很少。他们本打算只来一两年，赚一小笔钱就回去。谁会料到有这些困难？租金和生活费那么高，工钱却那么少。他们被迫出卖劳力，在贫困之中过日子，回不了家乡。

Colonel Fred Bee 中华执政官，旧金山，1884年

想当时，我们大多都忍着苦楚，强颜装欢，把眼泪往膝盖上擦。别人称我们为'coolie'，华文就是'苦力'。

Medical examination, Angel Island, San Francisco, early 1900s

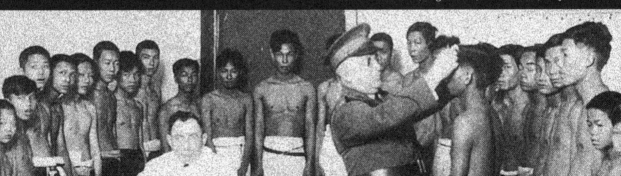

**In Australia and New Zealand, some newspapers carried
unflattering reports of us.**

They travelled in gangs of 20 to 200, carrying their gear on bamboo poles
slung over their shoulder, neither walking nor running but moving with
a short trot timed to the swing of the load, their loose shoes slapping
against the soles of their feet or dragging along the ground with a harsh
grating noise that provided a continuous accompaniment to their high
singsong voices.

Bathurst Free Press, 26 May and 1 September 1858

**Our arrival in the new land was met not by gold and joy,
but by confusion, exploitation, quarantine and humiliation.
Treated as commodities, our strength and labour were
traded for board and lodging. In the West Indies in the
nineteenth century, coolies were sold as slaves.**

...when offered for sale in the men-market we were divided into three
classes—first, second and third, and were forced to remove all our clothes,
so that our persons might be examined and the price fixed. This covered us
with shame.

The Cuban Commission Report: The Hidden History of the Chinese in Cuba, 1876

**In other parts of the world, coolies were indentured migrant
workers who contracted their labour in return for money.**

Many Chinamen have come, few have returned... They have expected
to come here for one or two years to make a little fortune and return.
Who among them ever thought of all these difficulties? Expensive rents,
expensive living though wages are low. Yet they are compelled to labour
and live in poverty, quite unable to return to their native land.

Colonel Fred Bee, Chinese Consul in San Francisco, 1884

**Most of us ate bitterness with a smiling face and wiped
our tears upon our knees. We were called 'coolie' by others,
which in Chinese is *kuli*, meaning 'bitter strength'.**

39

越南:一段悠长的历史

...华人售卖的商品种类多得惊人。房子都被隔成似乎一模一样的小隔,里面陈列着各种各样的货品-酱料、篮子、靴子、纸盒、刷子、蜡烛等等。在养鸭场,鸭蛋在铺满稻壳的孵化器具里;等蛋快要孵化时,就把它们放到一块薄纱上,不久之后,几百只小鸭就一起破壳而出。在一个稍显破旧的小屋里,玻璃工匠用一根长管吹着熔化了的玻璃液体,把它做成碗、杯子和灯罩。许多织布机塞满了其他屋子,织个不停...

法国旅者Robequain描述他在法属印度支那的Cholon的华人居社所见到的各种贸易和产业

华人在印支半岛的历史长达两千多年。早期华人中包括了艺人、贸易商和制造商,还有军人和官员。从公元前111年到公元939年,越南北部一直是中国的一个省,而中国移民则形成了社会中的上流阶层,把自己视为越南人。

经过几世纪,越南的国王和统治者一直尝试着控制这些移民,尤其是他们之中的商人。在越南北部地区,华商被限制于位于东京湾的**Van Dorn**岛屿做买卖,而成千上万的铜、铁、银矿工也不能走出边界的几个省份。在南部,华人人口到了18世纪时达到三、四万人。他们许多人是在满清政府征服明朝时逃难过来的,帮助了越南人把柬埔寨人从湄公河流域赶走。

到了1870年代,法国政府征服了越南南部后,开始侵入越南北部,遇到了越南人和华人的并肩反抗。1954年,法国军队最终撤出了越南,许多华人也从支持共产主义的北部逃到了南部。

1956年,西贡政府把所有在越南出生的华人都规定为越南公民。他们还必须取越南名字;这迫使许多华人不得不离开越南。1975年,西贡被越南北方政府的军队攻陷,离开越南的人潮也随着增加。新的越南共产政府没收了私人资产,逮捕了无数人;华人学校、报章和医院都被迫关闭。1978年到1989年之间,有超过一百万个难民离开了越南,其中65%是华人。如今,华人社群大多居住城市。

Vietnam: A Long History

...the variety of Chinese manufactures is extraordinary; there are buildings divided into seemingly identical compartments, which shelter the most diverse manufactures—food pastes, basketry, boots, paper boxes, brushes, candles etc. Here is a duck raising establishment where the eggs are put into incubators filled with paddy chaff; when ready to hatch they are set out on a piece of screen where hundreds of ducklings emerge cheeping from their broken shells. In an old shed, glassmakers are blowing paste through a long tube to make bowls, bottles and lamps. Elsewhere looms placed side by side operate in crowded rooms...

Traveller Charles Robequain on the activities of the Chinese in the Cholon-Saigon area, 1939

The Chinese have had a history in Indochina for nearly two millennia as artisans, merchants, soldiers and administrators. From 111 BC to AD 939, north Vietnam was a Chinese province, and the immigrants formed an elite that regarded itself as Vietnamese.

Over the centuries, various Vietnamese kings and overlords tried to control the immigrants, especially the traders among them. In the north, Chinese traders were only allowed to operate on Van Dorn, an island in the Gulf of Tonkin, and copper, iron and silver mineworkers were restricted to the border provinces. In the south, the Chinese numbered 30,000 to 40,000 by the eighteenth century. Many were refugees who had fled when the Manchu conquered Ming China, and they helped the Vietnamese to drive out the Khmer from the Mekong Delta.

When the French government, having taken over south Vietnam, began to encroach upon the north in the 1870s, they encountered resistance from both the Vietnamese and Chinese. In 1954, when French forces finally withdrew from Vietnam, thousands of Chinese fled the Communist north for the south.

In 1956, the Saigon government declared that all Chinese born in Vietnam were Vietnamese citizens and had to take Vietnamese names. This prompted many Chinese families to leave the country, a movement given impetus by the fall of Saigon in 1975. The Communist government confiscated properties and made numerous arrests, while Chinese schools, newspapers and hospitals were shut down. Between 1978 and 1989, a million refugees left the country, 65% of whom were Chinese. Today, the Chinese population is concentrated largely in Vietnam's cities.

南非：争取平等的斗争

英-布尔战争（1899-1902年）过后，南非的杜省地区完全毁于战火之中。矿场老板在英国殖民政府的许可之下，从中国招募了超过六万名契约工人。当地华人人数不断增加，引起了反亚情绪和1906年的'亚洲人登记法令'。这法令强制杜省地区的所有华人重新登记，而南非华人极力反对，认为这是对他们的极大侮辱，是奴隶的标志。华人社群在梁佐的领导下，和当时正在南非约翰内斯堡当律师的甘地所领导的印度社群一起参加了'不合作'抗议运动。梁佐和甘地1908年被判坐牢，而登记法令被通过，成了正式法律。

许多现在居住在南非的华人都是19世纪时来到南非的契约工人和商人的后代。在南非的种族隔离政策下，华人处于介于白人和黑人社会地位之间的边缘地带。华人没有投票权，被迫接受隔离开来的地区和设施。

到了1969年，华人被允许搬进其他种族地区行商定居，而1960年代到1980年代，华人逐渐被允许住进白人地区，进入白人占多数的学校和教堂。然而，超过60%的华人大学毕业生在这期间离开南非，移居别的国家。1990年代来到南非的华人移民改变了当地华人社群的构造，但华人仍占非洲人口的少数。

South Africa: A Common Fight

After the Anglo-Boer War (1899–1902), Transvaal mine owners, sanctioned by the British colonial government, imported more than 60,000 indentured Chinese labourers. The increased presence of the Chinese led to anti-Asian protests and the Asiatic Registration Act of 1906, which demanded the compulsory re-registration of all Asians in the Transvaal. The Chinese community protested against the Act as a gross indignity and a badge of slavery. Led by Leung Quinn, it joined the passive resistance movement of the Indian community under Mahatma Gandhi, who was a lawyer in Johannesburg. Leung Quinn and Gandhi were imprisoned in 1908, and the re-registration act was passed.

Many Chinese in South Africa today trace their descent to the indentured labourers and merchants who arrived in the nineteenth century. Under apartheid rule, the Chinese occupied a marginal position between the whites and the blacks. They had no voting rights and were subjected to separate living areas and amenities.

In 1969, the Chinese were allowed to move into other racially defined areas for trade and residence, and from the 1960s to the 1980s, they were permitted to live in white areas and attend predominantly white schools and churches. However, more than 60% of Chinese graduates left South Africa during this period for other countries. New Chinese immigrants who arrived in the 1990s have redefined the community, though the Chinese still form a minority of the country's population.

Pioneers

**Our forefathers went overseas
to seek their fortunes and carried
with them the expectations and
hopes of entire families.**

到海外闯事业的先辈们背负了全家
人的希望与期待。

燕鹊喜，
贺新年；
爹爹去金山赚钱，
赚得金银成万两，
返来起屋兼买田。

自从奔异地。
落拓在花旗。
屈指算来年卅岁。
求谋未遂待乘时。
今得志。
财神跟住尾。
洋蚨富足荷包里。
整定归鞭有日期。

Plantation workers, Malaya, late 1800s/early 1900s

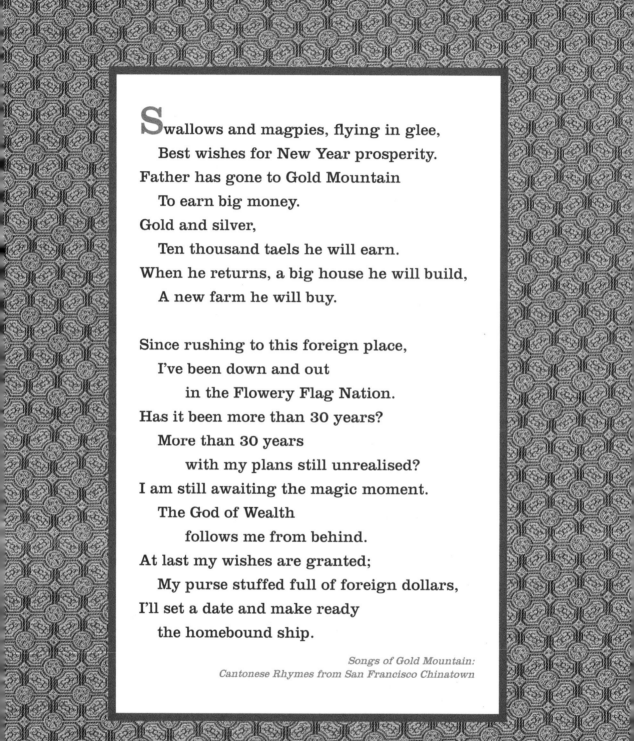

Swallows and magpies, flying in glee,
   Best wishes for New Year prosperity.
Father has gone to Gold Mountain
   To earn big money.
Gold and silver,
   Ten thousand taels he will earn.
When he returns, a big house he will build,
   A new farm he will buy.

Since rushing to this foreign place,
   I've been down and out
        in the Flowery Flag Nation.
Has it been more than 30 years?
   More than 30 years
        with my plans still unrealised?
I am still awaiting the magic moment.
   The God of Wealth
        follows me from behind.
At last my wishes are granted;
   My purse stuffed full of foreign dollars,
I'll set a date and make ready
   the homebound ship.

Songs of Gold Mountain:
Cantonese Rhymes from San Francisco Chinatown

Miners leaving
Flemington, Australia,
for the goldfields, late
1800s/early 1900s

Coolies receiving their contracts, Southeast Asia,
late 1800s/early 1900s

extraordinary fortitude

Those who left were ordinary men with extraordinary
fortitude. Before the God of Wealth granted their
wishes, they toiled under trying conditions and had
to battle not only the harshness of nature and the
unfamiliar terrain, but also persecution at the hands
of local communities.

They were chased out of towns. At times, they had to
vacate mining areas for white miners. In America in
1856, the residents of Mariposa County, California,
ordered the Chinese to leave: 'Any failing to comply
shall be subjected to 39 lashes, and moved by force of
arms'. In El Dorado County, angry white miners set
fire to the tents and equipment of the Chinese miners,
and turned back stagecoaches filled with Chinese
passengers. In Los Angeles in 1871, 22 Chinese were
killed by mobs that attacked a Chinese section of
the city. In Wyoming in 1885, the residents of Rock
Springs killed 28 Chinese coalminers, mutilated their

Plantation workers, Delhi, India, c. 1870

Tobacco factory workers, Delhi, India, c. 1905

超凡毅力

到海外的，都是拥有超凡毅力的普通人。在财神爷实现他们的心愿之前，他们在极其恶劣的条件下奋斗，不但得在陌生的土地上和残酷的自然环境搏斗，还得面对当地人的咄咄逼人。

他们被逼着离开。有时，他们被迫把好矿地让给白人矿工。1856年的加里福尼亚州马利普萨县，当地居民命令所有华人离开："违命者将被鞭打39下，并将被强行驱离。"在艾多拉多县，愤怒的白人矿工放火焚烧华人矿工的帐篷和开矿器具，并阻止载有华人的马车进入县里。1871年的洛杉矶，一群暴徒袭击了华人区，造成22个华人身亡。1885年，怀俄明州石泉镇的白人居民杀害了28名华人煤矿工人；他们肆意毁坏他们的尸体，焚烧了他们的木屋。

Tobacco plantation with supervisor, Delhi, India, c. 1905

The Australian goldfields, c. 1850

turning dirt into gold

Denied the best land, Chinese miners became scavengers who worked abandoned claims. Through hard work and patient toil, they were able to extract the last bit of gold that remained. Eventually, their ability to do so won the grudging admiration of other miners.

The Chinese are first-rate scavengers. They sweat all the gold out of the ground whereas the Europeans do not; the Chinese get some gold out of old forkings and tailings, a good deal by taking the bedrock deeper... The Europeans, as a rule, think that the ground is in runs, and when the yield falls off on the sides, they consider it useless to proceed any further in that direction but push ahead; whereas the Chinese take out the whole of the wash and consequently the whole of the gold, hence their success.

As a case in point, I may mention the Anglo-Swiss claim (Upper Waikaia) that was purchased by the Chinese a little over two years ago, since which time fully 5,000 ounces of gold have been taken out of a very small area of the claim.

The Tuapeka Times, 10 September 1884

There are quite a number of Chinamen engaged in mining on the river bars. Many bars have been worked and abandoned, and others have not been worked, owing to the difficulty of getting water to them... In the construction of these works, they often display much ingenuity and knowledge of hydraulics.

TW Symons, *Symons Report on the Upper Columbia River and the Great Plains of Columbia*, 1882

Inverell, Australia, c. 1925

There is a well-known story about a miner named Ah Sam who bought a dirt-floored log cabin from six American miners for $25. They thought he was a fool. Ah Sam suspected that there was gold in the cabin because the previous owners had been careless, and had let gold dust fall all over the floor. Ah Sam and his mates carefully washed the dirt in the entire cabin, and from an investment of $25, Ah Sam made a profit of $3,000. For every Ah Sam who prospered through luck and sheer hard work, there were thousands of others who succeeded through their skills and sense of entrepreneurship.

Their energy and enterprise have made the Malay States what they are today... They were already miners... before the white man had found his way to the peninsula. In all the early days it was Chinese energy and industry which supplied the funds to begin the construction of roads and other public works, and to pay all the other costs of administration... They brought all the capital into the country when Europeans feared to take the risk... They introduced tens of thousands of their countrymen when the one great need was labour to develop the hidden riches of an almost unknown and jungle-covered country, and it is their work, the taxation of the luxuries they consume and of the pleasures they enjoy, which has provided something like nine-tenths of the revenue.

Sir Frank A Swettenham, Malaya, 1906

Goldminers, America, late 1800s/early 1900s

淘土成金

华人矿工没有最好的矿地，只能到废弃的矿场做拾荒者。通过艰苦而耐心的劳作，他们取出残存的金子。最终，华人从废弃矿地中提取金子的本领使得白人不得不对他们刮目相看。

中国人真是一流的废物利用专家。他们把欧洲人没有提取到的金子一点不剩地从地下提取出来；他们从残渣碎石中提取金子，挖深岩床找到更多金子。欧洲人通常会认为这块地方已经荒废了，当矿道矿石产量减少时，他们觉得再挖下去也没用，于是转而往前方挖掘；可中国人不一样，他们把矿场淘个精光，因而淘光了所有的金子，所以会成功。就像是两年前中国人买下的英瑞矿场（威凯亚上段）；到目前为止，只是从这个矿场的其中一小块地方，他们就淘出了整整5,000盎司的金子。

Tuapeka Times 1884年9月10日

有许多中国人在沙洲上挖矿。这些沙洲许多是被挖掘过后遗弃的；另外那些没有被挖过的是因为把水输上去有困难...在做这些工程时，中国人时常会表现出其独特的创造力和高超的水利学造诣。

Mount Ida, Otago,
New Zealand, c. 1900

TW Symons, *Symons Report on the Upper Columbia River and the Great Plains of Columbia*, 1882年

有个广为人知的故事说道：一个叫 Ah Sam 的矿工，花了25美元向六个美国矿工买下了一间建在泥土地上的木屋。他们都认为Ah Sam是蠢材。其实，木屋的原主个个粗心大意，所以Ah Sam 猜他们一定是让很多含有金子的矿土都落在木屋泥地上。Ah Sam 和伙伴们仔仔细细地把木屋里的泥土地淘了一遍，而25元的投资，换来的是价值 3,000 元的金子。每出一个像 Ah Sam 一样靠运气与努力成功的，就有几千个其他人，凭着自己的技术、创业精神和什么工作都肯做的态度而成功。

他们的努力与积极进取，造就了今日的马来亚...他们早在白种人登上马来半岛前已经在此开矿了...早期时候，正是华人的努力和他们创办的产业为建造公路以及其他公共建设提供了资金，并承担起了各种行政费用...在欧洲人不敢到此冒险的时候，是他们把资金注入了这个国家...当深藏于这个少为人知、丛林密布的国家里的沃土最需要人力来开拓时，是他们带来了成千上万个同乡；是他们的劳作、消费和享受时所缴交的税，构成了这国家九成左右的收入。

Sir Frank A Swettenham, Malaya, 1906年

Miners, South Africa, c. 1905

Molyneux River, Otago, New Zealand, c. 1901

Market
gardener and
goldminer,
Otago, New
Zealand, c. 1903

Members of the Chinese Labour Corps working on an airfield, France, World War I

Processing gambier, Riau, Indonesia, c. 1900

Salmon cannery, British Columbia, Canada, c. 1887

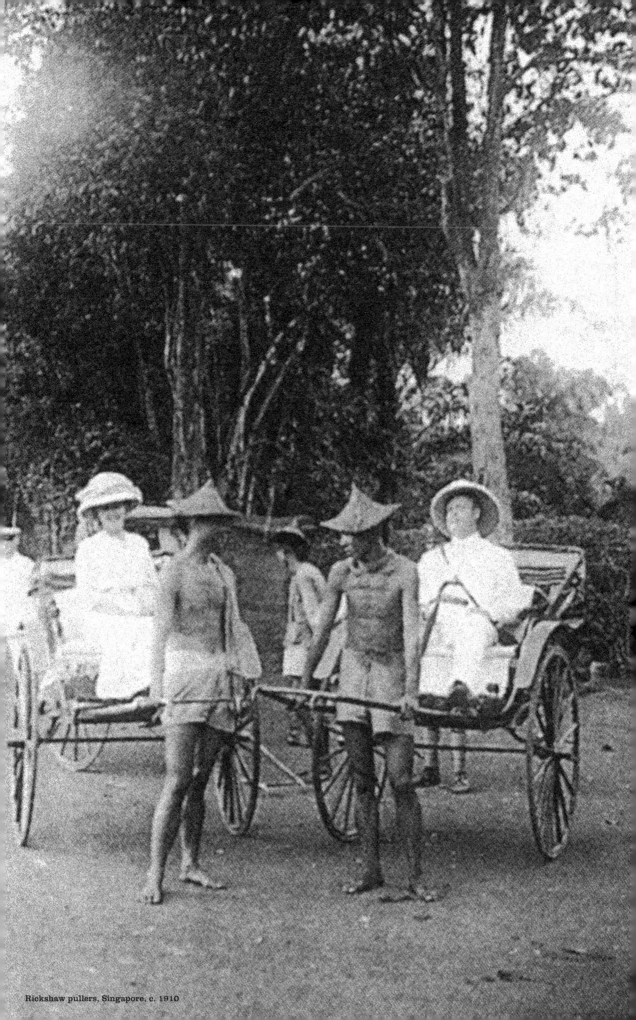

Rickshaw pullers, Singapore, c. 1910

reshaping the gold mountain dream

In every foreign land, Chinese sojourners had to reshape their dreams and expectations and adapt to new conditions. They survived by doing all sorts of work, no matter how difficult, dirty or lowly. Sam Suk, a tin miner in Malaya in the early 1900s who, late in life, became a butcher, typified the spirit of the Chinese overseas. He said, 'With two hands and two feet, we knew we would never starve. You work hard, have courage and endurance, you will live'.

Amongst no people does the transformation from the labourer to the artisan class take place with such rapidity.

Charles A Winchester, British Consul, Xiamen, 1852

There is no place where you do not find the Chinese.
From the sacking of guano, to the cultivation of the valleys;
From waiting at the tables to cleaning the streets.
He is even the servant of the commoner, and there is no activity—
You understand?—on which he does not diligently embark.

Juan de Arona, Peruvian poet, late 1800s

The Chinese overseas have a saying that they teach their children: 'To succeed in life, learn to eat bitterness'. Such fortitude helped them to bear hardship and loneliness on foreign shores. Although thousands had started out as poor coolies, many did not remain so for ever. The next mountain was always higher than the one they were on, and they climbed onwards and upwards. As a common Cantonese expression says, 'With no fear of the sky above, and no fear of the earth below', they sailed the oceans and criss-crossed the earth. Unafraid of toil and pain, these ordinary sons and fathers made good in the new lands.

Tea peddler, Hawaii, c. 1912

重塑金山梦

无论在海外哪个地方，华人都得重新塑造自己的梦想和期望，尝试适应新环境。为了谋生，不论是多难、多脏、多低微的工作，他们都做。沈素是1900年代初到马来亚的锡矿工人，后来成了肉商；他就是海外华人奋斗精神的典型范例。他曾说：'只要有手有脚，我们就饿不死。只要你用功做事、勇敢、有耐性，就能活下去'。

没有哪个民族如此快速地从劳力阶层上升为艺术阶层。

Charles A Winchester, 厦门的英国执政官, 1852年

无地不见华人：
他收捡鸟粪，
他谷中种耕；
他桌边侍应，
他大街扫尘。

他甚至是普通人的下人。
这世上没有任何工作－任何！
你明白吗？—他不愿担任。

Juan de Arona, 秘鲁诗人, 1800年代末

海外华人教导儿女时有这么一句话：'吃得苦中苦，方为人上人'。正是这种坚忍不拔的品格帮助了他们克服在海外的艰辛与孤苦。虽然多数人开始时是当苦力的，但许多人并没有当一辈子的苦力。人总是往着更高的山上爬去。他们前进、上升。就如广东俗语所说，'上不惧天，下不畏地'，他们越洋过海，足迹遍布天下。这些普通的儿子们和父亲们，不畏艰辛，在新天地里实现了自己的理想。

Members of the Chinese Labour Corps involved in non-combatant work, World War I

Vineyard workers, Southern California, late 1800s/early 1900s

bush-clearers

In Australia in the 1850s, thousands of Chinese coolies were employed to clear scrub and bush. They opened up virgin lands and did tree-felling, ring-barking and scrub-cutting. In Cairns, the Chinese pioneered a technique for felling rows of trees, bringing them down like dominoes. One well-known bush-clearing pioneer was Jimmy Ah Kew of Wahgunyah. He began as a coolie and became the headman of 500 Chinese labourers clearing bush in an area that covered hundreds of miles.

gardeners and farm workers

...in the theatre of agriculture, the Chinese have the front seat while the whites sit behind them and admire their pigtails.

The Cairns Post, 22 May 1889

The American west,
late 1800s/early 1900s

Chinese market-gardeners in New South Wales and Victoria contributed substantially to the Australian diet... By providing fresh vegetables, Chinese gardeners kept scurvy at bay; and by honest toil, they turned wasteland into productive areas...

Moreover, Chinese gardeners also contributed to European landowners who benefited in at least two ways—the collection of rents and the utilization of their land... Many humble gardeners were popular and remembered with gratitude in country districts. In 1907 in a Victorian town, a Chinese market gardener known as Ah Louy, after 25 years labour in that district, decided to return to China. On the eve of his departure, the local Australian population held two farewell parties at the town hall in his honour. At the first party, 253 ladies were reported to have witnessed the presentation of a gold watch to the bewildered guest who had done an invaluable service to the local community.

The Chinese Australian Herald, 15 June 1907

Whoever goes to the outskirts of the city will perceive at the ends of unfinished streets, on the hills, valleys, and slopes, on the roadsides, in fact, everywhere, small vegetable gardens encircling the city with one belt of greenness. The ant-like labor of the Chinese has transformed the sterile sand into the most fertile black earth... The fruits and vegetables, raspberries and strawberries under the care of the Chinese gardeners grow to a fabulous size. I have seen strawberries as large as small pears and heads of cabbage four times the size of European heads, and pumpkins the size of our wash tubs.

Nobel Prize-winning writer Henryk Sienkiewicz
on the market gardens of San Francisco, 1955

Coming as they did from small villages in coastal southern China, they brought with them centuries-old skills in tropical horticulture, introducing irrigation technology and new fruit and vegetables that greatly diversified the diet of Northern Queenslanders open to culinary experimentation.

Henry Reynolds, *North of Capricorn: The Untold Story of Australia's North*

Horticulturalists, Otago, New Zealand, c. 1903

Pepper plantation workers, Singapore, c. 1890

Otago, New Zealand, c. 1902

Otago, New Zealand, late 1800s/early 1900s

Orange pickers, Santa Ana,
Orange County, California,
c. 1895

Tobacco plantation, Southeast Asia, c. 1870

拓荒者

1850年代的澳洲，成千上万的华人受雇清树开荒。他们开发荒地，砍伐树木、剥去树皮、斩除灌木。在北澳的凯恩斯，华人首创了一种清树方法，把树整排推倒。其中一位拓荒先锋是华根也的 Jimmy Ah Kew。他是苦力出身，后来成了带领500名华工的工头；他们在成百英里的土地上清树开荒。

菜农与农场工人

...在农艺这个大戏院里，中国人占据了前排；白人只能敬陪末座，瞻仰他们的辫子。

The Cairns Post，1889年5月22日

新南威尔斯和维多利亚州的华人菜农对澳洲的饮食做出了不可磨灭的贡献...他们供应了新鲜蔬菜，人们得以避免患上坏血症；他们勤奋的劳作，把荒地化成了沃土...除此之外，华人菜农还在至少两方面使欧裔的农场主获益：农场主们可以收取土地租金，土地也充分地被利用...许多身份卑微的菜农在乡村地区广受欢迎，人们感激他们、怀念他们。1907年，在维多利亚州的小镇上，有个叫Ah Louy的菜农。他在那儿经过了25年的耕耘后，决定回返中国。在他临走的前一天晚上，当地的澳洲居民在镇公所为他举办了两场欢送会。有253位女士在第一场欢送会上亲眼见证到这位不知所措的嘉宾被授予一枚金表，以表彰他为当地镇民做出的重大贡献。

The Chinese Australian Herald，1907年6月15日

去到市区周围的人都应该察觉到：一个个小菜园遍布在未完工的街道顶端、小山上、山谷里、山坡上、道路旁，或应该说，所有地方；它们形成一条绿色的腰带，环绕着整个城市。华人像蚂蚁一般的勤劳已经将这片荒芜的沙丘变成了肥沃的黑土地...不论是水果还是蔬菜，黑莓还是草莓，华人种植的东西总是大得让人惊奇。我见过像小梨子一样大的草莓，比欧洲菜头大四倍的菜头，和像脸盆一样大的南瓜。

诺贝尔得奖作家 Henryk Sienkiewicz 描述旧金山的市场菜园，1955年

他们来自中国南部海岸线上的小村庄，带来了在那儿流传了好几世纪的种植技术和引水灌溉技术。他们还引进了新品种的瓜果蔬菜；对乐于尝试新奇食物的北昆士兰人来说，这使他们的生活饮食生色不少。

Henry Reynolds, *North of Capricorn: The Untold Story of Australia's North*

Pepper plantation, Singapore, c. 1890

A doctor and his attendants, Australia, c. 1879

labourers

The most enterprising miner in this district is Ping Que, an intelligent Chinaman who speaks good English. He employs about 14 coolies.

John Knight, Secretary to the Government Resident, *New Territory Times*, 27 May 1876

Besides being a miner, Ping Que was an astute businessman in the Northern Territories, Australia. He was known for his industry and integrity. Mastering the English language, he teamed up with European partners to expand his mining operations. He also opened stores and butcher shops, constructed sheep and cattle pens and slaughtering places, and owned 600 head of cattle. In 1878, when Australian teamsters charged £45 a ton and more for freight from Southport to Pine Creek, Ping Que employed 100 coolies to do so, charging lower rates. This forced the teamsters to reduce their charges, and helped reduce transport costs.

Members of the Chinese Labour Corp on the Western Front, c. 1917

Labourer with his equipment, Australia, late 1800s/early 1900s

货运工人

在这地区（联合区）里，开矿人之中最有企业精神的是平鹊。他是个聪明的中国人，说着一口流利的英语，雇佣了大约14个苦力。

John Knight, *New Territory Times*, 1876年5月27日

除了开矿之外，平鹊也是精明的商人，勤奋与正直人所共知。他精通英语，可以和欧洲人合作扩大矿场经营。他也开办商店、肉店、建立养羊场、养牛场、屠宰场，养的牛多达600头。1878年，当澳洲的卡车司机从 Southport 运货到 Pine Creek 收费是一吨45英镑时，平鹊雇佣了100 个苦力来运货，采用较底的价格收费。结果这迫使了卡车司机调低收费，运输费也因此下降了。

The Central Pacific Railroad, at the foothills of the Sierra Nevada Mountains, c. 1870

Preparing explosives for extending the railroad, California, c. 1889

railroad builders

At the peak of railroad construction in America during the late 1800s, the Central Pacific Railroad Corporation employed more than 10,000 Chinese railroad builders. These men cut tunnels through the rugged Sierra Nevada Mountains and lay train-tracks across the deserts of Nevada and Utah. They were organised into teams of ten to 20, each with a cook and a headman, and their wages were $30 to $35 a month, the same as a white labourer. The Chinese builders cooked their own food and had special ingredients such as abalone, bamboo shoots, dried oysters and mushrooms brought by wagon from San Francisco.

Charles Crocker, one of the 'Big Four' partners of the Central Pacific Railroad Corporation, defended his employment of Chinese builders: 'Any race that could build the Great Wall of China could build a railroad!' When the Irish labourers of the rival Union Pacific Railroad set a record for laying eight miles of track in one day, Crocker's Chinese workers bested that record on 28 April 1869 by completing ten miles of track in a single day.

On May 10, 1869, when the railways from the east and west were finally joined at Promontory Point, Utah, the Central Pacific had laid 690 miles of track and the Union Pacific 1,086 miles. The two coasts (of America) were now welded together. Before the transcontinental railroad, trekking across the country took four to six months. On the railroad, it would take six days. This accomplishment created fortunes for the moguls of the Gilded Age, but it also exacted a monumental sacrifice in blood and human life. On average, for each two miles of track laid, countless workers perished in accidental blasts. Eventually more than 1,000 Chinese railroad workers died, and 20,000 pounds of bones were shipped back to China. Without Chinese labor and know-how, the railroad would not have been completed. Nonetheless, the Central Pacific Railroad cheated the Chinese railway workers of everything they could. The Chinese workers were not only excluded from the ceremonies, but from the famous photograph of white American laborers celebrating as the last spike, the golden spike, was driven into the ground. Of more immediate concern, the Central Pacific immediately laid off most of the Chinese workers, refusing to give them even their promised return passage to California. The Company retained only a few hundred of them for maintenance work, some of whom spent their remaining days in isolated small towns along the way, a few living in converted boxcars. The rest of the Chinese former railway workers were now homeless as well as jobless, in a harsh and hostile environment.

Iris Chang, *The Chinese in America: A Narrative History*

The Transvaal, South Africa, c. 1907

华人建筑工人得挖隧道贯通崎岖的 **Sierra Nevada** 山脉，在内华达州和犹他州的沙漠上铺设铁轨。在铁路建设的高峰期，中央太平洋铁道公司雇佣了超过一万名华工。他们10到20人组成一队，每队配有一名厨子和工头。他们每月的工资是30到35美元，和白种工人拿的一样。他们煮自己的食物，食物里有从旧金山用马车运来的特殊材料，像鲍鱼、芦笋、干蚝和蘑菇。

Charles Crocker 是中央太平洋铁道公司的四大合伙人之一。他为公司雇佣华人劳工作出自辩：'能够修筑起万里长城的民族，当然可以修筑铁路！' 当竞争对手联合太平洋铁道公司的爱尔兰工人创造了一天内铺设八英里铁轨的记录时，1869年4月28日，Crocker手下的华人劳工以一天铺设10英里铁轨的成绩打破了这项记录。

1869年5月10日，从东方和西方两边铺设过来的铁路在犹他州的 **Promontory Point** 连接上了；中央太平洋铁道公司铺设了690英里的铁轨，联合太平洋铁道公司铺设了**1,086**英里。（美国的）两边海岸现在被焊接起来。在有这条横贯大陆的铁路之前，从东岸到西岸得花四到六个月的时间；现在坐火车只花六天。这成就为黄金时代的大亨们带来了巨额财富，但也牺牲了无数鲜血与生命。平均说来，每铺设两英里铁路，就会有意外造成无数员工死亡。最终有超过一千名华人建筑工身亡、超过两万磅的骨灰被运回中国。没有华人劳工的辛劳和技艺，就没有这条铁路。虽然如此，中央太平洋铁道公司还是欺骗华人建筑工。他们不止不让华人建筑工参加庆祝活动，就连那张最后一个铁钉被打入土时，白人工人在庆祝铁路建成的照片里，华人工人也没有出现。中央太平洋铁道公司随即马上解雇了大部分的华人劳工，也没有支付给他们曾应允过的回加里福利亚的路费。公司只留了几百个华人劳工负责维修工作；他们一些在铁道旁偏僻的小镇上、另一些在改装的火车厢里度过了人生剩下的日子。其他以前的建筑工无家可归，也没了工作，等待他们的只有残酷的现实环境。

Iris Chang, *The Chinese in America: A Narrative History*

Railroad builders, Vancouver, British Columbia, Canada, c. 1880

Removing timber, Sumatra, c. 1921

Shopowner, America, c 1910

entrepreneurs

**A Hawaiian-born Chinese in the 1930s described how
Chinese migrants switched from coolie labour to trading.**

Wong Ah Fook

Even though the Chinese emigrant has been a farmer, or a worker
around the village, nearly every one of them has had some experience
at bargaining. I know for instance that my folks used to go into Macau
about once a week to peddle their produce. Peddling has been taken up
as a sort of secondary occupation. Many of the families have little or no
land; there may not be enough land to keep the whole family busy. Some
of the individual members will try selling something in order to make
money. When they go overseas, many of them soon get into peddling and
hawking... The peddler gets a little money and buys a box of fruit, some
peanuts, and then he carries them around selling them. When he has been
at it a while, and has saved some money, he gets a cart and increases his
stock. Eventually he may set up a small shop.

Clarence E Glick, *Sojourners and Settlers: Chinese Migrants in Hawaii*

**In 1854, at the age of 17, Wong Ah Fook came to Singapore.
He was a carpenter's apprentice for some years, then went
into building construction. He secured a contract to build
two godowns, and from his contacts with Hoo Ah Kay
(Whampoa), one of the most prominent businessmen at the
time, he became a supplier to the British navy. He helped
found the first Chinese bank in Malaya, and is remembered
as one of the pioneers who develop Johore.**

In my life I have gone to the South Seas by myself and endured much
hardship and suffering in Singapore and Johor...

Wong Ah Fook, *Guangzhou Will*

Trader, Vancouver, British Columbia, Canada, c. 1926

Traders with coolies, Jakarta, Indonesia, c. 1875

企业家

1930年代，一个出生于夏威夷的华人描述了华人移民怎么从苦力变成商贩。

华人移民，不论是农夫还是村子里的打工仔，多少都有讨价还价的经验。比如说，我家人以前大概每个星期都会去澳门售卖他们种出的农作物。于是沿街叫卖就成了第二职业。许多家庭都只有一小块地，或根本没有；家里的地根本不够让全家人去种。有些家庭成员就会卖东西赚点钱。他们去到国外，很多人就会开始卖东西，做生意…商贩有了点钱，就买上一盒水果，四处叫卖。不久之后，存下了一些钱，就会买推车，多买些货物。最后他还可能开店铺。

Clarence E Glick, *Sojourners and Settlers: Chinese Migrants in Hawaii*

黄亚福是广益银行的创始人。十七岁的他1854年到了新加坡，当了几年木匠学徒，之后做起建筑生意，还获得建造两间仓库的合约。他和当时的大商胡亚基（Whampoa）建立起了业务往来，因此得以进入其他领域，还成了英国海军的供应商。他后来和其他人合作创建了马来亚第一家华人银行。他也被认为是发展柔佛州的先驱。

我曾独身下南海，在新加坡和柔佛州吃过很多苦…

黄亚福

加勒比群岛和南美洲:散种

加勒比群岛

19世纪初,英属东印度公司的'刚毅号'轮船载了200名华人劳工到达加勒比群岛从事制糖种植园的工作。接下来的70多年,有超过二十万名华人契约劳工被招募到各个受英国控制的岛屿,如古巴、英属圭亚那、牙买加和英属洪都拉斯,或受法国控制的马提尼克岛和瓜达卢佩。

> 在古巴,华人得日日夜夜不停地干活,不能享受一丝安宁。不仅如此,我们还时常被毒打,我们所受的待遇和牛、马、羊、狗一样…
>
> 《古巴委员会报告:被隐藏的古巴华人历史史》,1876年

古巴委员会发现,在40,327名华人之中,只有66名女性。许多华人男子娶了当地女性,而如今加勒比混血华裔中包括了世界知名古巴艺术家Wilfredo Lam和圭那亚古典钢琴家Ray Luck等人。

秘鲁

上千个华人苦力在秘鲁参与建造安第斯铁路,还有一些则在利马南边的鸟粪肥料场工作丧命。长达8年的卖身劳工契约,几乎和当奴隶没什么区别,而契约期常被强制性延长。那些熬过契约期活下来的华人劳工,定居于秘鲁的沿海各省,成了自由劳动者。在亚马逊地区发现了金矿和橡胶,吸引了更多华人在那儿定居。

墨西哥

在巴西和墨西哥的华人暂居者大多在沿着铁路和矿区的工业市镇定居,从事着投资兴建的城镇所需要的各种业务。1800年代末,华人富商在瓜伊马斯和埃莫西约开店;到了1900年代,他们控制了大多数杂货和食品贸易。1920年代至1930年代,反华运动造成华人被趋赶,通婚被禁止,墨西哥的华人人口因此减少了。二战之后,来自中国大陆、台湾、香港和澳门的华人移民陆续又回到墨西哥。

The Caribbean and South America: Scattered Seeds

The Caribbean Islands

In the early 1800s, the *Fortitude*, an English East India Company ship, brought 200 Chinese workers to the Caribbean to work on sugar plantations. Over the next 70 years, more than 200,000 indentured labourers went to British-controlled Cuba, British Guiana, Jamaica and British Honduras, or French-controlled Martinique and Guadalupe.

The Chinese in Cuba have to labour night and day, and do not enjoy one instant's tranquillity; we are in addition constantly beaten and treated in every way like oxen, horses, sheep or dogs...

The Cuba Commission Report: A Hidden History of the Chinese in Cuba, 1876

The 1876 Cuba Commission Report also found that there were only 66 Chinese women in a Chinese population of 40,327. Many Chinese men married local women, and among Caribbean Chinese of mixed parentage today are Cuban artist Wilfredo Lam and Guyanese classical pianist Ray Luck.

Peru

In Peru, thousands of Chinese coolies toiled to build the Andean railroad and died in the guano mines south of Lima. Their eight years of indentured labour was akin to slavery, and this period of service was often forcibly extended. Those who survived their servitude settled on the coastal provinces to work as free labour. The discovery of gold and rubber in the Amazon further attracted Chinese to settle there.

Mexico

Chinese sojourners in Brazil and Mexico settled mainly in working-class settlements near railways and mining areas, catering to the needs of towns that rose because of new investment. In the late 1800s, Chinese merchants opened stores in Guaymas and Hermosillo, and by the 1900s, controlled much of the trade in general goods and foodstuffs. In the 1920s and 1930s, anti-Asian campaigns led to the expulsion of Chinese and a ban on Chinese-Mexican marriages, and the Chinese population in Mexico declined. After World War II, immigrants from China, Taiwan, Hong Kong and Macao began to arrive again.

南太平洋地区：一串小社群

19世纪时，为了寻找檀香、海参、龟壳、珍珠这些贵重物品，许多富于冒险精神的中国人坐船到了斐济、巴布亚新几内亚、所罗门群岛和大溪地。来自悉尼和广东的华商在太平洋岛屿上设立贸易中转站，许多人也娶了当地女性，发了财，供养着他们在中国和南太平洋的家庭。1865年到1941年间，大约有两万名华人到了椰子乾核和香蕉种植园当契约劳工。

斐济

1900年，在斐济只有大约100个华人居住。之后，当地香蕉贸易的增长吸引了更多华籍劳工，华人社群在两次世界大战之间壮大了。太平洋战争期间，华人靠供应商品给军人富裕起来。这吸引了更多华人移民，而如今在斐济大约有五千名华人，大多住在苏瓦。

巴布亚新几内亚

在巴布亚新几内亚最早出现的华人移民像在南太平洋其他地区的华人一样，也是来自广州和福建的契约劳工。有些是从澳洲来的，少数成了富商，在中国和澳洲有家族联系。当地1,500名华人，一部分出生于当地，是早期华人居民的后代，另一部分是从印尼、马来西亚、香港和台湾来的新移民。曾三次担任过巴布亚新几内亚总理的陈仲民爵士是具有华人血统的混血儿。

法属波利尼西亚

法属波利尼西亚包括众多岛屿，但大多数人都住在大溪地，包括华人在内。1855年，来自澳洲的广东金矿工人前往加利福尼亚途中路经大溪地。他们在当地定居；十年后，一千多名客家契约劳工也到了。种植园倒闭时，他们多数回了中国，但有些选择留下来。如今的华人在零售业界十分活跃。早期的华人居民大多娶了当地女性，而多年来，原本很小的华人社群在1990年代增加到了将近九千人。

The South Pacific:
A String of Small Communities

In the nineteenth century, Chinese seekers of sandalwood, *beche-de-mer*, tortoiseshell and pearlshell sailed to the South Pacific in search of these prized commodities. Chinese traders from Sydney and Guangzhou set up trading stations on Pacific islands, and many took local wives and became wealthy, with families in China and the South Pacific. Between 1865 and 1941, about 20,000 indentured labourers also arrived to work on copra and banana plantations.

Fiji

In the 1900s, there were only about 100 Chinese on Fiji. Later, the growing trade in bananas brought more workers, and the community thrived in the years between the two World Wars. During the Pacific War, the Chinese prospered through businesses that supplied the military. This success attracted more Chinese immigrants and today, there are about 5,000 Chinese in Fiji, mostly in Suva.

Papua New Guinea

Like most of the Chinese in the South Pacific, the first Chinese settlers in Papua New Guinea were indentured Cantonese and Hakka labourers. Some of these workers had emigrated from Australia, and a number became wealthy traders with family networks in China and Australia. The Chinese population of 1,500 is divided between local-born descendants of the early settlers and new arrivals from Indonesia, Malaysia, Hong Kong and Taiwan. Sir Julius Chan, thrice the prime minister, is of mixed ancestry.

French Polynesia

French Polynesia comprises numerous islands, though most of the population (including the Chinese) live on Tahiti. In 1855, Cantonese goldminers from Australia stopped at Tahiti on their way to California. They decided to stay and ten years later, were joined by 1,000 Hakka indentured labourers. When their plantation went bankrupt, most of them returned to China, though some chose to stay. Today, the Chinese are active in the retail sector. Most of the early settlers married local women, and over the years, this small population had increased to almost 9,000 in the 1990s.

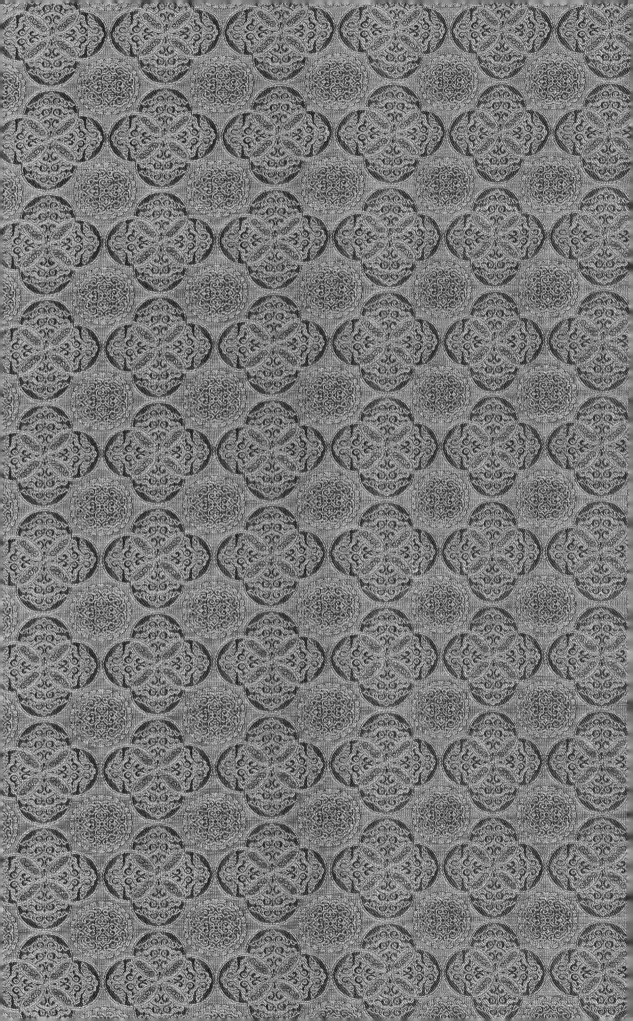

Chinatown

In the early 1900s, Chinatown was seen as by outsiders as either an exotic place or a ghetto riddled with crime and vice. But for Chinese sojourners during this period, at the height of anti-Asian feelings, the Chinatowns in America, Canada and Australia were places where they were protected and could wander the streets safely.
For them, Chinatown was home.

1900年代初期，外人把唐人街看成是个古怪诡异的地方，或是充满着罪恶、污秽和堕落的贫民窟。不过，在这反亚情绪达到高潮的时期，美国、加拿大和澳洲的唐人街成了旅居海外的华人的避风港。他们被保护，可安全地上街走动。对他们来说，唐人街就是家。

Dupont Street, Chinatown in San Francisco, late 1800s/early 1900s

Ross Alley, Chinatown in San Francisco, late 1800s/early 1900s

The gate to Chinatown, Jakarta, Indonesia, c. 1901

through different eyes

On the eastern side of the city, but outside of it and in front of its walls, at the distance of a musket-shot, is a silk market which they call Parián. Usually 15,000 Chinese live there; they are Sangleys, natives of China, and all are merchants and artisans. They possess, allotted among themselves by streets and squares, shops containing all kinds of merchandise and all the trades that are necessary in a community. The place is very orderly and well arranged, and a great convenience to the citizens.

Franciscan monk Bartholomé de Letona on Manila's Chinatown, 1661

It is as if a little East-Asiatic township, by some magic power, had been transplanted to New Britain... There are half a dozen stores there, several restaurants, tailors, laundries and bootmakers; butchers, bakers, carpenters, mechanics etc ...Although most of the shops neither impress by size nor cleanliness, but are just what one would expect in a Chinese quarter, there is plenty of excuse for everybody to go there... Over and above all, Chinatown is Rabaul's busy, unruly corner – where people rise early—are always on the move—and go to bed late. While after sunset the European quarter becomes quiet, and the streets look empty and desolate, life in Chinatown moves on—intense—rapid—and wicked.

Australian soldier James Lyng on Rabaul's Chinatown, New Guinea, 1919

The Chinese quarters are some of the most interesting sights of the city. Endless rows of open shops, line the streets on either side, with the family wash stretched on bamboo poles, suspended from the upper windows.

Every other shop appears to be a restaurant. The Chinese—like the French people—take most of their meals outside their homes. Innumerable children play around, and on the pavements, pariah dogs prowl about, looking for scraps; placid mothers sit outside nursing their quaint babies, and groups of young men may be seen watching, with keen interest, games of cards in progress.

Margaret Wilson on Singapore's Chinatown, 1934

During the 1800s and up to the Second World War, many Westerners saw Chinatown as a ghetto, strange and crime-ridden. To the Chinese, however, especially the earliest generation of immigrants, Chinatown was more than a collection of streets and shops; it was a sociocultural space that offered a way of life reminiscent of the homes they had left behind.

The American west, late 1800s/early 1900s

Lynn Valley, British Columbia, Canada, c. 1905

Chinatown in Rabaul, Papua New Guinea, c. 1933

Chinatown in Singapore, late 1800s/early 1900s

仿佛是东亚的某个小镇被魔术般地移到了英国…那里有半打杂货店、许多餐馆、裁缝店、洗衣店、鞋店、肉铺、面包店、木工坊、五金店…尽管大多数店铺给人的印象是并不是很宽敞很干净，但华人的地方本来就是这样的。有很多很充分的理由让大家都愿意到那去…最重要的是，唐人街是 **Rabaul** 市里最繁忙、最喧腾的地方－那里的人们起得早、睡得晚，整天忙碌个不停。天黑后，当欧籍区里全都沉静下来，街道上冷冷清清时，唐人街里的人的活动仍然继续着－依然还是那样紧张、快速而邪恶。

澳洲军队的澳洲人 **James Lyng** 描述 **1919** 年新几内亚 **Rabaul** 的唐人街

华人住的地区可以算是这座城市里最有趣的地方了。数不清的店铺排列在街道两旁；楼房里一根根竹竿从楼上的窗子里伸出来，上面挂满了洗好的衣服。

每家店铺旁边都可以看到饭馆。和法国人一样，中国人绝大多数时候选择在外面而不是家里用餐。数不清的小孩子在街边玩耍嬉戏。行人道上，野狗在寻找着食物。妇女毫无避忌地坐在户外给婴孩喂奶。还可以看到很多年轻人围在一起看别人打牌。

英国作家 **Margaret Wilson** **1934** 年在新加坡旅游时描述当时的"牛车水"（新加坡的唐人街）

从 **1800** 年代到二战之前，西方人把唐人街看成是贫民窟，是一个诡异而充满罪恶的地方。但对于海外华人，特别是对于第一代的华人移民，唐人街并非仅是地图上的一个地区的名称；它是一个华人社会、文化的空间集合；在它里面的生活可以让他们回味起他们离开了的故乡的生活。

Chinatown in Singapore, c. 1900

Balloon vendor, Dupont Street, Chinatown in San Francisco, late 1800s/early 1900s

Chinatown, America, late 1800s/early 1900s

Amah with child, Dupont Street,
Chinatown in San Francisco, late
1800s/early 1900s

Street market in Chinatown, Singapore, c. 1910

Chinatown in Sacramento, California, c. 1896

Huie Kin, a sojourner who came to San Francisco in 1868, remembered San Francisco's Chinatown:

...[it] was made up of stores catering to the Chinese only... Our people were all in their native costume, with queues down their backs, and kept their stores just as they would in China, with the entire street front open and groceries and vegetables overflowing on the sidewalks. Forty thousand Chinese were then resident in the bay region, and so these stores did a flourishing business.

Knut Dahl, a scientist visiting Northern Australia in the 1890s, also found much to admire in Darwin's Chinatown. He compared it to the European part of the city, saying:

The few business people and officials in the service of the Government were apparently in no hurry over their duties and adopted the cool and indolent habits peculiar to the majority of white men in tropical towns. Little or no life appeared in the streets, everybody knew everybody else, and the resident Commissioner was generally mentioned by his Christian name.

Chinatown, on the other hand, was a welter of life and activity. The very air smelt of business. You heard, saw and felt nothing but business. One had the feeling that the people one saw thronging the shops and streets, who bought and sold, and, busy as ants, carried on their trades, belonged to a race which slowly and securely was gaining opulence and power. In Palmerston Chinatown, one might fancy oneself in a modest business quarter of one of the towns of the Far East. Only late at night did the business life of the streets cease. Then crackers were burnt in honour of the gods or to scare away devils, and red tapers were lit in front of the houses. And large gongs and drums were heard throbbing in the Temple.

And in the light galvanised iron houses sat Chinese families... They were happy. They had religion, sympathy and unity.

Chinatown in Vancouver, British Columbia, Canada, c. 1890

Huie Kin是**1868**年到了旧金山的旅居者。在他记忆里，唐人街是个与上述完全不同的地方：

> 旧金山的唐人街有许多只卖华人物品的商店...就像在中国，我们都穿着自己家乡的服饰，束辫子，开店铺。整条街的店铺都敞开了门，杂货和菜就摆在街道走道上。当时有四万个华人住在海湾一带，因此这些店铺的生意都好得不得了。

1890年代到访北澳的科学家**Knut Dahl**也觉得达尔文城市的唐人街有许多可赏之处。他把唐人街与城市的欧洲区作比较：

> （欧人区里）寥寥可数的一些生意人和为政府工作的官员，好像对自己的工作并不着急。他们沾染了热带地区大多白人都有的冷酷、怠惰的习惯。街道上基本上没什么人走动。大家都互相认识，亲昵地用名字来称呼当地的行政官。

> 相反的，唐人街里生气盎然，连空气里都弥漫着做生意的气息。听到的、看到的、感觉到的，全都是生意。可以感觉得到，这些在拥挤的商店和街头做着买卖、像蚂蚁一样忙碌着赚钱的人，一定属于一个缓慢而稳健地积累着其财富和权力的社群。站在**Palmerston**的唐人街里，就像是到了远东某个中等发达商业地区的城镇一样。大街上的买卖活动只有到了深夜才停止；接着人们就会燃放鞭炮，祈求神灵保佑或是驱赶鬼怪；屋子门口也会点起红蜡烛；还可以听到庙里传来的锣鼓声。

> 而华人家庭就住在那些铁皮屋里。他们生活很愉快，他们有自己的信仰，富有同情心，很团结。

Boarding house, Gulgong, New South Wales, late 1800s/early 1900s

Chinatown in Vancouver, British Columbia, Canada, c. 1926

Gamblers, Singapore, late 1800s/early 1900s

China, late 1800s/early 1900s

three evils: gambling, opium and prostitution

Tempted by dreams of instant wealth, desperate men often fell prey to gambling. A great attraction in Chinatown were the gambling houses where men could play dominoes, dice, cards and ancient games such as *fan-tan*, *pak-a-pu* and *pye que* (a game of dominoes). The popular press termed these gambling places 'dens'.

'Den' is described in the dictionary as: a wild animal's home; a place in which to take shelter or hide; (figurative) a place where thieves or their like have their headquarters; (figurative) a small, dirty or neglected room or dwelling. The images provided by the press and court records helped to perpetuate the stereotypical alien image of Chinese and were an effective tool for whipping up anti-Chinese sentiment.

Jan Ryan, *Ancestors: Chinese in Colonial Australia*

The English East India Company brought large quantities of opium to China through the port of Guangzhou. The use of opium soon spread through every strata of society, and immigrants brought the habit with them when they went overseas. The British government derived a portion of its revenue from opium monopolies in its colonies, and in Singapore alone in 1923, there were 423 government-run opium shops.

Opium smokers, Singapore,
late 1800s/early 1900s

The smoking room measured about 60 feet by 20, and accommodated a hundred men without overcrowding. A shallow gully marked the centre of the dirty floor.

Two wooden benches, six feet wide, were built one above the other against the side-walls, and ran the length of the building. These benches were neither screened from the room nor divided into cubicles, so that smokers lay in long rows, cheek by jowl, with their feet towards the gully.

Policeman Alec Dixon, describing an opium shop, 1920s

Mounting international criticism against opium led to anti-opium campaigns, some of which were spearheaded by Chinese merchants and Christian churches, though commercial greed and individual addiction had already created what many Chinese regarded as an endemic social disease in Chinatowns all over the world.

Chinatown, America, c. 1900

Lonely men in Chinatown also found relief in the arms of a woman. For a fee, a man could buy a woman's body for a short period. It was a commercial transaction. In California in 1852, there were seven Chinese women and 11,794 Chinese men—a ratio of 1,685 men to 1 woman. In 1870, there were 63,199 Chinese in America, only 4,566 of whom were female—a ratio of 14 to 1.

During the Great Depression, tour operators exploited such stereotypes in Chinatown like the slave girl, *tong* gangster and sinister characters like Fu Manchu. Chinatown was touted as an exotic destination for white Americans, and busloads of them toured Chinatowns in San Francisco and New York. Chinese residents, exasperated by the lies of tour operators, fought back.

We hated them! Because the sightseers, they would come around, they would always be talking bad stories about China... [Chinese come to the United States to] make a living, not to capture white girls for slavery! (I yelled)... We would have fights with them. How many times I go up there, I say That's a lie! And then I hit them!

Lung Ching, New York's Chinatown, 1915

三恶：赌、烟、嫖

陷入困境的人常受发横财的诱惑而沉迷于赌博。吸引最多人的是那些提供骨牌、纸牌及包括诸如 fan-tan、pak-a-pu 和 pye que（骨牌赌博游戏）等古老赌博游戏的赌场。大众媒体把这些赌场称为 'den'。

'Den' 在字典里的解释是：野兽的住处；可以避难或躲藏的地方；（比喻）盗贼的总部；（比喻）窄小、肮脏、不起眼的房间或屋子。媒体和法庭记录所呈现的影像加深了华人是异族的印象，成了制造反华情绪的有效工具。

Jan Ryan *Ancestors: Chinese in Colonial Australia*

英国东印度公司通过广州这海港将鸦片运入中国。鸦片很快地就蔓延到中国的各个阶层。出国的华人移民把抽鸦片的恶习也带到了海外华人聚居的地方。英国殖民政府垄断了其殖民地里的鸦片市场，并从中获得了巨大的商业利益。1923年时，单是在新加坡，当地政府就开办了423家鸦片馆。

烟馆房间大概有60尺长、20尺宽，可以毫不拥挤地容纳下一百个人。在肮脏的地板中央有条浅浅的小沟渠。

房间两边各有两条六尺宽的长凳叠在一起靠着墙摆放着，长度和整间屋子一样。这些长凳并没有被用屏风遮起来，也没有隔成小间的房间。吸大烟的人一个个横躺在长凳上，脚对着沟渠。

警察 Alec Dixon，描述鸦片馆，1920年代

全球性的反对鸦片的声浪不断增大，引发了好几次反鸦片运动，其中几次就是由一些华人富商和基督教堂发起的。鸦片生意所带来的巨大商业利润，以及其能让人上瘾的特性，使得鸦片演变成为世界各地的唐人街里的社会弊疾。

孤身男人在女人的怀抱里获得舒解。只要付一笔钱，男人就可以暂时买下一个女人的身体。这只是一场商业交易。1852年的加利福尼亚州，共有七名华人女性和11,794名华人男性，男女人数比例是1,685:1。1870年，在美国的华人中有63,199名男性，只有4,566名女性，比例是14:1。

世界大萧条时期，旅游观光公司为了赚钱，利用了唐人街里低俗的典型人物－女奴、妓女、黑帮分子和不切实际的人物，如Fu Manchu。他们把唐人街描述成一个奇异而邪恶的旅游景点，穿行于旧金山和纽约的唐人街的旅游巴士上载满了来观光的美国白人。导游们和旅游公司的谎言激怒了美国华裔，使得他们开始反击。

我们恨他们！因为那些来观光的，总是说我们中国的坏话。'（在美国的华人）是来谋生的，不是来抢白人女孩做奴婢的！'（我朝他们叫道）...我们会和他们打起来。我好几次上前去说：'那是假的！'然后我就打他们。

Lung Ching，纽约的唐人街，1915年

Prostitute, America, late 1800s/early 1900s

意中人隔远。独自倚栏看。
几回恼煞月团圆。令我肠回更九转。

挂胆肝。痴情难割断。
怎得重逢同作伴。免吾寡宿枕衾寒。

My loved one is far away.
   Alone, by the railing,
      I look around aimlessly.
Many times, depressed by
   a bright, full moon,
My body aches and twists
   with ninefold grief and pain.

A heart left hanging.
   A deep love that cannot be severed.
Just how can we be reunited
   and share companionship again?
Spare me from sleeping
   with only a cold quilt and pillow.

Songs of Gold Mountain:
Cantonese Rhymes from San Francisco Chinatown

three pleasures: meeting friends, opera and dining

For overseas Chinese men in Sydney, Melbourne, Wellington, San Francisco or New York in the early 1900s, the three pleasures of Chinatown were meeting friends, opera and dining. Imagine yourself in a land where no one understood you, and you were ridiculed because you wore your hair differently or spoke a language they couldn't understand. What a relief it would be to walk into a place where you were welcomed, and where you didn't have to strain to make yourself understood.

Most of us can live a warmer, freer, and a more human life among our relatives and friends than among strangers… Chinese relations with the population outside Chinatown are likely to be cold, formal, and commercial. It is only in Chinatown that a Chinese immigrant has society, friends and relatives who share his dreams and hopes, his hardships and adventures. Here he can tell a joke and make everybody laugh with him; here he may hear folk tales told and retold which create the illusion that Chinatown is really China.

Ching Chao Wu, 1928

Children, Chinatown in San Francisco, c. 1924; musician, Chinatown in San Francisco, c. 1925

In Chinatown, the overseas Chinese could buy herbs and medicines, foodstuff such as noodles, dried mushrooms, and century eggs. This was where they could remit money, send letters home or simply yarn the hours away with their clansmen. The letter-writer was likely to be a book-keeper or a clerk in a store, such as the herbal shop. Sometimes he was the caretaker of the temple or the clan association. For a small fee, he would read aloud the letter that your family had sent you, or write one for you to send home.

He tells the writer of the letter what he wants said. Perhaps he can only send a little money this time: he has been out of work; times are hard; he wishes he were able to send more money. Sometimes the letter is written as the man dictates; sometimes the writer listens and then writes it later. These writers know what the proper things are to say and what this man's folks will like to hear.

Young Hing-cham, 1932

Dazzling performances by opera troupes were one of the great delights in Chinatown, especially during the festive seasons like the Lunar New Year. There were also teahouses and restaurants where one could go for *dim sum* or tea.

Street opera, Singapore, c. 1890

Chinese theatre

Children in holiday wear, Chinatown in San Francisco, late 1800s/early 1900s

三乐：会友、看粤剧、用餐

对**1900**年代初住在悉尼、墨尔本、威灵顿、旧金山或纽约的海外华籍男子来说，唐人街里有三大乐趣－会友、看粤剧和用餐。设想身处在一个没有人明白你的陌生国度：就因为你的发型和本地人不同，或是因为你说的话别人听不懂，而被人嘲笑。在这个时候，走进一个人们欢迎你、不须要为别人听不懂你而心烦的地方，这是一件多么惬意的事。

> 我们大多数人在和亲戚朋友在一起时，会比和陌生人一起时过得温馨、自在、感觉有人情味。华人和不属于唐人街的人之间的关系大多很冷淡、客套而且商业化。只有在唐人街里，华人才能找到伙伴、亲戚、朋友，和他们一起分享他们的梦想与希望、他们的烦恼与经历。在这里，他可以讲出大家都会笑的笑话；在这里，他可以听到一讲再讲的中国民间故事；这些都可以让他感到似乎这里就是中国。
>
> Ching Chao Wu, 1928年

海外华人能在这些地方买到草药、中药以及华人的食物，如面条、干菇、咸蛋、皮蛋之类的。华人可以在这里汇钱、寄信回家，或与同乡逛逛街，打发时间。

'信佬'大多是记账人，或是像中药店这样的店里的书记员。有时寺庙或是同乡会馆里的主事也会做'信佬'。你只要付一小笔钱，他就把家人写来的信念给你，或是帮你写信寄回家。

> 他把想要跟家里人讲的话告诉信佬：他这次可能只能汇一点点钱回家；他失业了；在这边的生活很艰难；他本来希望自己可以多汇一些钱回家的...有时信佬就照原话边听边写下来；有时他先听完之后才写信。信佬知道这信该怎样写，明白寄信人的家人想听什么样的话。
>
> Young Hing-cham, 1932年

观看粤剧团的精湛表演是唐人街里的赏心悦事之一，尤其是在像农历新年这样的节庆时候。唐人街里有许许多多的茶馆和餐馆，人们经常到那里吃点心、饮茶。

Storefront notices, Chinatown in Milan, Italy

Remittance clerks, Chinatown in Singapore, mid 1900s

Street market, America

Storefront notices, Chinatown in Milan, Italy

菲律宾：变化与过度

早在西班牙人**1570**年到达菲律宾之前，华人移民与商人就已造访当地。到了**19**世纪，他们的后代在菲律宾群岛的发展中扮演着重要的角色。在西班牙人统治时期，约有两万名华商、店主和工匠生活在马尼拉。**17**至**18**世纪，西班牙人和华人之间互不信任，引发了许多动乱。当地华人因此被隔离到称为'八连'的地区。许多人这时改用菲律宾式姓名。像 **Tanjuatco, Cojuangco, Ongpin, Limjap** 和 **Yangco** 等菲律宾姓氏都是华人改称的姓氏。

尽管这段崎岖坎坷的历史，菲律宾华裔 **Jose Ignacio Paua** 被认为是**1890**年代菲律宾革命运动的英雄；华菲混血儿埃米利奥·阿吉纳尔多将军是菲律宾第一共和国的总统；许多菲律宾的重要人物，如菲律宾民族运动的英雄扶西·黎刹医生，以及主教辛海棉，都有华菲混血血统。

1930年代至**1970**年代，即使在菲律宾出生成长的华人，也并不被承认是菲律宾公民。直到**1975**年，菲律宾政府改变了政策，才使得大量菲律宾华人得以加入菲律宾籍。**2001**年，菲律宾总统格罗利亚·马卡帕加尔·阿罗约造访了马尼拉唐人街，成为菲律宾历史上第一个正式造访唐人街的总统，由此翻开菲律宾华人史上新的一页。

The Philippines:
Changes and Transitions

Chinese sojourners and traders arrived at the Philippines
before the Spanish in 1570. By the nineteenth century,
their descendants were playing an important role in the
development of the islands. Under Spanish rule, 20,000
Chinese lived in the Manila area as traders, shopkeepers
and craftsmen. In the seventeenth and eighteenth centuries,
mutual distrust between the Spanish and the Chinese led to
uprisings and the Chinese were segregated into quarters
called *parian*. Many changed their names during this
period, and Filipino surnames with Chinese origins include
Tanjuatco, Cojuangco, Ongpin, Limjap and Yangco.

Despite this history, José Ignacio Paua, an ethnic Chinese,
is regarded as a hero of the Filipino Revolution of the 1890s.
General Emilio Aguinaldo, a mestizo, was the President
of the First Philippines Republic, and many prominent
Filipinos including Dr José Rizal and Cardinal Jaime Sin
are of mixed ancestry.

From the 1930s to 1970s, the Chinese were not regarded
as Filipino citizens, even if it was the land of their birth.
It was only from 1975 onwards that a change of policy has
enabled the mass naturalisation of Chinese Filipinos. In
2001, President Gloria Macapagal-Arroyo made history by
becoming the first Filipino president to pay a formal visit
to Manila's Chinatown.

印度尼西亚：期待未来

荷兰人16世纪到达印尼时，在爪哇和苏门达腊这些港口城市里已经存在着繁荣的华人聚居地。这些早期华人之中，有的是娶了当地女性的回教徒，他们的领袖被印尼统治者指定为'syahbandars'－意为'港口的主人'，代表统治者向当地人收税。

现代印尼华人包括两种：土生华人和'新客'。土生华人是早期华人居民和印尼'原住民'女子的后代。'新客'华人则是在19世纪末来到印尼的华人移民的后代，保留了中国传统语言和习俗。如今这两种华人之间的区别已较模糊。

19世纪时，荷兰殖民政府在华人劳工和商业企业的帮助下为印尼建立起了贸易和农业种植业。他们和印尼统治者一样，任命华人领袖为'甲必丹'，负责维持法治、秩序，收取税金。'甲必丹'如张鸿南、张煜南、许金安、黄仲涵等，构成华人社会中的上流阶层。

成千上万的华人死于日据时期和其他政治动乱时期。直到近期，印尼华人都没有获得公民权。他们不能教授华语；店铺标志上禁止书写中文；许多华人改取了印尼名字。

现在情况有了变化。华人又开始在雅加达的唐人街里庆祝春节，开始学习融入印尼社会，尝试多元文化，以寻求印尼人民的认同。印尼华人对美好未来的期望，表达在诗集《以睫毛支撑世界》里。

> 我等你接纳我，
> 已三十年；
> 还不太迟
> 我只要一丝希望。

Indonesia: A Hopeful Future

When the Dutch arrived in Indonesia during the sixteenth century, there were already thriving Chinese settlements in the port cities of Java and Sumatra. Some of these early Chinese were Muslims who had married local women, and their leaders were appointed *syahbandars* (masters of the ports), and collected taxes on behalf of the rulers.

The Chinese community in Indonesia consists of two groups, the Peranakans and the Totoks. The Peranakans are descendants of the early settlers who married *pribumi* (indigenous) women. The Totok Chinese are descended from settlers who came in the late nineteenth century, and who have retained their Chinese language and customs. Today, differences between the two communities are less distinct.

In the nineteenth century, the Dutch authorities used Chinese labour and commerce to open up the country for trade and agriculture. Like the Indonesian rulers, they appointed Chinese *kapitans* (headmen) to maintain order and collect taxes. During Dutch rule, *kapitans* like Tjong Ah Fie, Tjong Jong Hian, Khouw Kim An and Oei Tiong Ham formed an elite within the economy.

Thousands of Chinese died during the Japanese Occupation of World War II and as the country underwent periods of turmoil. Until recent times, Chinese Indonesians were denied citizenship and could not teach Chinese. Chinese shop signs were banned, and many Chinese adopted Indonesian names.

But things are changing. Chinese New Year is once again celebrated in Jakarta's Chinatown, and many seek acceptance through inclusion and multiculturalism. This hope for a better future is expressed in an anthology by Chinese-Indonesian poets entitled *Menyangga Dunia di atas Bulu Mata (Supporting the World on an Eyelash)*, written in Chinese and Indonesian.

Menanti engkau	I've been waiting for you
Selama tiga puluh tahun	For thirty years
Tak juga terlalu terlambat	It's not yet too late
Kau meraup untukku—harapan	You grab for me—hope

Yenny, *Kau Berasal Dari Angkasa Luar: You Come from Outer Space*

Women

In times of hunger and pestilence, we, China's worthless daughters, were sold overseas as prostitutes and bondmaids. But those of us who were strong-willed left our villages of our own accord to work as labourers and servants.

当饥荒和瘟疫肆虐时，我们这些'没用的女儿'们被父母卖到国外当妓女、丫鬟。我们之中也有一些人个性坚强、独立；她们选择自己离开家乡，到国外去当建筑女工或女佣。

Brothels in San Francisco Chinatown,
late 1800s/early 1900s

苦相身为女，卑陋难再陈。
男儿当门户，堕地自生神。
雄心志四海，万里望风尘。
女育无欣爱，不为家所珍。

傅玄，公元200-300年

How sad it is to be a woman!
   Nothing on earth is held so cheap.
Boys stand leaning at the door,
   Like gods fallen out of heaven.
Their hearts brave the Four Oceans,
   The wind and dust of a thousand miles.
No one is glad when a girl is born;
   By her the family sets no store.

Fu Xuan, AD 200–300

A prostitute, San Francisco,
late 1800s/early 1900s

unwanted

In the nineteenth century and earlier, girls born into poor families in China were often killed, abandoned or sold as bondmaids, concubines and prostitutes.

...in China, girls were considered useless and I recall the many babies left on the road in the vague hope that someone might adopt them. It was not unusual to find a baby wrapped in a blanket and left on the roadside. The usual procedure was to unwrap the blanket, have a look at it and, if it were a boy, to claim him at once as an adopted son; but if it were a girl, a cent would be placed nearby and she would be left for the next passer-by to do the same. At times many cents surrounded a girl baby and I was told that sometimes greedy people would carry her home with the money, and then keep the money and throw the baby out. In the winter most of these babies die soon after they had been abandoned.

An elderly Chinese woman, Singapore

prostitutes

From the 1850s to the early 1900s, Chinatowns all over the world were mainly bachelor societies in which the men were married but alone, with few women living among them.

A prostitute, San Francisco,
late 1800s/early 1900s

- **Mauritius, 1881**
  Out of 3,549 Chinese residents, 9 were women.

- **New Zealand, 1881**
  Out of 4,995 Chinese residents, 9 were women.

- **Singapore, 1893**
  Out of the 189,843 Chinese passengers who arrived that year, 9,640 were women.

- **Hawaii, 1900**
  Out of 25,767 Chinese residents, 3,471 were women.

- **The US mainland, 1900**
  Out of 89,863 Chinese residents, 4,522 were women.

- **Madagascar, 1904**
  Out of 443 Chinese residents, 3 were women.

- **Korea, 1910**
  Out of 11,818 Chinese residents, 1,089 were women.

- **France, 1911**
  Out of 13,084 Chinese residents, 139 were women.

Politicians in cities like San Francisco and governments such as the British regarded prostitution as a necessary evil, and brothels (*loh kui chai*) flourished in Chinatowns across America and Asia.

遗弃

19世纪以前，在中国出生于穷人家的女孩，不是被杀掉或丢弃，就是被卖去当丫鬟、小妾或妓女。

...在中国，女孩被视为没用的废物。我记得很多人把刚出生不久的婴孩遗弃在路旁，希望有人收养。路旁包着婴儿的包裹屡见不鲜。通常路人会打开包裹看一下；如果是男孩，就带回家收养；但如果是女孩，他们就会在她身旁放上一枚铜钱，留给下一位路人来决定要不要收养。有时，放着女婴的包裹边上会摆放了很多铜钱；听说有些见钱眼开的人会把女婴连人带钱拿回家，然后留下钱，再把女婴丢掉。冬天时，被遗弃的婴孩通常很快就会被冻死。

海外妓女的故事

从1850年代到1900年代，世界各地的唐人街社会里大部分都是单身汉；他们其实都结了婚，却一个人生活，女性非常少。

- 毛里求斯，1881年
  有3,549名男性华人，只有9名女性

- 纽西兰，1881年
  4,995名华人居民当中，只有9名女性

- 新加坡，1893年
  那年有189,843名华人到过新加坡，其中只有9,640名是女性

- 夏威夷，1900年
  25,767名华人之中，只有3,471名女性

- 美国本土，1900年
  89,863名华人居民当中，只有4,522名女性

- 马达加斯加，1904年
  有443名男性华人，只有3名女性

- 朝鲜，1910年
  11,818名华人居民当中，只有1,089名女性

- 法国，1911年
  有13,084名男性华人，只有139名华人女性

住在如旧金山城市里的政治家，以及许多殖民地政府当局，包括英国人，都把娼妓这行看作是必存的社会弊病，而妓院在美国与亚洲的唐人街十分普遍。

Arrival of
Cantonese women
in Singapore,
c. 1930

蒙污青楼处。节烈尽丧除。
最耻同人来接臂。任教旅客舞全躯。
姜豫推。益觉羞难语。
拼命要离花粉队。
跟个好佬乐唱随。

Prostitute
Chinatown in Sa:
Francisco, lat
1800s/early 1900

A green mansion is a place of
   filth and shame,
   Of lost chastity and lost virtue.
Most repulsive is it to kiss
   the customers on the lips,
   And let them fondle
   every part of my body.

I hesitate, I resist;
   All the more ashamed
   beyond words.
I must by all means leave
   This troupe of flowers and rouge;
Find a nice man and follow him
   as his woman.

Songs of Gold Mountain:
Cantonese Rhymes from San Francisco Chinatown
('green mansion' refers to a brothel)

Polly Bemis, Idaho, late 1800s/early 1900s

a pioneer of the american west

Polly Bemis' life began in northern China in 1853. She was sold to bandits for two bags of seed and eventually travelled to America. In 1872, a saloonkeeper in an Idaho mining camp bought her, giving her the name Polly. Some time later, a miner named Charlie Bemis won her in a poker game.

Polly used her knowledge of herbal medicine to heal Charlie's wound from a gunfight, and they married and settled on a plot of land on the Salmon River. Polly saved her husband's life a second time by dragging him from their burning cabin. Homesteaders would seek Polly's help for illnesses and wounds, and when she died in 1933, she was one of the most respected citizens of Grangeville. The townspeople named the stream running though her property Polly Creek.

a hope of making good

Who wants to be a prostitute all their lives? Many women trapped into prostitution sought escape by looking for a good man who could buy them out of the brothels. In San Francisco, the Presbyterian Mission Home rescued more than 1,500 girls, while in Malaya in 1885, the Poh Leung Kuk was set up to protect women and children. It also rescued many girls who had been sold into prostitution. These girls were given an education to prepare them for new and better lives.

拓荒于美国西部的人

Polly Bemis 的人生从1853年中国北方开始。她以两袋谷种的价钱被卖给土匪，后来被送到美国。1872年，在爱达荷某个矿区经营酒吧的一个华人老板把她买下了，为她取名为Polly。不久后，一个叫Charlie Bemis 的矿工在一次扑克牌局里赢了她。

Polly以她的药物知识把Charlie在枪支搏火中所受的伤医好。Charlie娶了她，两人住在Salmon河边的一块地。又有一次，她把Charlie从燃烧的木屋里拖出来，第二次救了他的命。当地居民们生病、受伤都求助于Polly，而她1933年过世时，已成了Grangeville镇上最受人敬重的人物之一。镇民为了纪念她，把流过她家土地的小河取名'Polly Creek'。

从良的希望

谁想当一辈子的妓女？许多不得已深陷其中的女子试着找寻出路，想找到一个愿意替她赎身、娶她的好男人。

旧金山的长老传教会救助了超过1,500个女子脱离苦海。1885年，在新加坡和马来西亚设立了'保良局'，专门保护女人、孩子。这机构救助了许多被卖入火坑的年轻女子脱离娼妓生涯。这些女子之后被送去接受教育，以便使她们准备过美好的新生活。

New Zealand, late 1800s/early 1900s

Amah and ward, Singapore, early 1900s

amahs and *ma chehs*

Amahs were Cantonese domestic servants from Guangdong
who worked in Hong Kong and Malaya. *Ma chehs* were
domestic servants from the Shunde District in Guangdong
who took a vow of celibacy. As part of their work, *amahs* did
all kinds of household chores, in addition to minding the
children and cooking, especially in less well-to-do families.
Amahs would refer to themselves with wry humour as *yat
keok tek* ('one leg kicks all').

I have mostly worked for Chinese families as a *yat keok tek*, which
included cleaning, washing, ironing, cooking, in fact everything except
minding the children. Most of the families had around six to seven
members. I woke up early in the morning around 5 a.m. and after getting
myself ready, I would start getting breakfast. The master left for work
after breakfast. After doing the dishes, I swept and cleaned the house from
top to bottom. When that was done, I washed the clothes and prepared
lunch, which the master would come back for. After clearing up, I did the
ironing. When that was done, I took a bath. It would then be time to cook
again. By the time dinner was over and I had cleared up and finished the
dishes, it would be about 9 p.m. I would be free then.

Tang Ah Tye

Amah 'sisters', with jewellery painted on the photograph for sending home, Singapore, early 1900s

'阿嬷'和'妈姐'

'阿嬷'指的是从广东出来到香港、马来亚、新加坡等地工作的家庭女佣。'妈姐'特指那些来自广东顺德县的女佣,她们选择'梳起',发誓终身不嫁。阿嬷除了看孩子、煮饭之外,还得做其他各种家务,尤其是在不富有的家庭。那些什么家务都做的阿嬷嘲讽地称自己为'一脚踢'。

> 我多数时候都在华人家庭里当'一脚踢'。家务包括了打扫、洗衣、烫衣、煮饭,其实就是除了看孩子之外,什么都做,大多家庭都有六到七个成员。我早上大约五点左右就起身,梳洗过后就开始准备早餐。雇主吃过早餐后就去上班。我洗过碗碟之后,就把整座房子从上到下里里外外打扫干净。之后我就洗衣服,然后准备午饭。雇主一家会回来吃午饭。午饭后收拾完东西,我就烫衣服。这些都做好之后,我就洗澡。然后又到了煮晚饭的时间了。晚饭过后,我收拾完东西、洗好了碗碟,时间就已经是晚上九点左右了。直到那时我才有空。

Tang Ah Tye

虽然所有的阿嬷都穿'衫裤',妈姐穿的是特别的白色衫裤上衣和黑色裤子。她们以流利的广东腔、彬彬有礼的态度和漂亮的外表而出名。她们穿的衣服的质地比一般阿嬷的好:上衣以上等细麻线或薄纱做成,裤子是缎子做的。她们不穿木屐鞋,而是黑色的平底套鞋。她们将自己的长发编成一条辫子,垂在身后。

> 我在一家有五个成员的英国家庭做'一脚踢'。他们煮自己的饭菜,不需要我为他们准备;但其他的事情全都是我做-打扫、洗碗、看孩子等等。我早上五点起床打扫屋子。所有东西都必须刷得干干净净、擦得亮堂堂的-真是很辛苦。他们在八点左右吃早餐。之后男主人就出去上班。两个年纪大点的孩子去上学,我就陪着那个小的玩、照顾他,直到午饭时间。大约一点左右,两个大点的孩子回来了。我热好午饭让他们吃。午饭过后,三岁的那个小的睡午觉,其他两个大的自己玩。这时候我才有时间煮我自己的饭。吃完了饭、洗了碗,我就洗衣服、烫衣服。当小的那个醒了后,我就带着三个孩子去外面的花园散步,到吃晚饭时回来。两个做父母的每天晚上都出去,要到凌晨两三点钟才回来。这段时间我就一直在家照顾小孩子。

Kwan Ah Sap

她们是个性坚强、生活节俭、拥有经济独立的女性。有了自己劳力赚来的钱,她们懂得照顾自己。有些退休时,还拥有地产。即使健康情况欠佳,她们仍然很坚强,不会自怨自艾。

> 人生短暂,有什么好伤心的? 何不把心思放在工作上? 有东西吃就吃,这就是我的生活方式...最重要的是有善良、慈悲的心...不管你得到多少,又不能带进棺材...最好不用依靠任何人。我从来没向人借过钱,哪怕是五分钱都没有。钱多点,就多花一点;没什么钱,就节省一点。我不求人,不欠任何人东西。

Tong Yuet Ching

Amah and ward, Singapore, early 1900s

Amah 'sisters', Singapore, c. 1988

While all *amahs* wore samfoos, *ma chehs* wore a distinctive white samfoo top and black trousers. They were known for their manners, stylish appearance and polished Cantonese. Their clothes were of better quality than those of other amahs. Their samfoo tops were of lawn or voile and their black trousers were satin. Instead of clogs, they wore black low-heeled shoes. Their long hair was worn as a single plait that hung down their back.

I worked as a *yat keok tek* for an English family of five. I didn't cook, they did it themselves, but I did everything else—cleaned, washed dishes, looked after the children and so on. I'd wake up at 5 a.m., then start cleaning. Everything needed to be scrubbed and polished. It was really hard work. At about eight, they'd have their breakfast. The husband would then go to work. The two older ones would be at school and I would play with and look after the little one till about lunch time, around one when the older children came home. I would prepare and give them their lunch. After lunch, the three-year-old took a nap while the older ones played by themselves. I would only then have time to cook and eat my own food. When that was over and the dishes had been done, I did washing and ironing. When the youngest one woke, I took all three for a walk to the Gardens and then back for dinner. The parents went out every night till about 2 or 3 a.m. and I was left looking after the children.

Kwan Ah Sap

Ma chehs were strong, frugal and financially independent women. With income from their own labour, they knew how to take care of themselves. A few, when they retired, owned property. Even in ill-health, they were indomitable and refused to give in to self-pity.

Man's life is short. What is there to be sad about? So why not spend your mind on your job? When there is food to eat, you eat. This is my way of life... The most important thing is to have a kind and compassionate heart ... no matter how much you get, you will never be able to bring to the coffin... It is good not to have to rely on others. I have never borrowed even five cents from anyone. If I have more money, I would spend more. If not, I would be more thrifty. I don't bother people and I don't owe anybody anything.

Tong Yuet Ching

Singapore, c. 1938

Samsui women, Singapore

samsui women

The Samsui women were another group of strong-willed
Cantonese women from the Upper Shanshui District of the
Pearl River Delta. Because of floods and famine in their
villages, they came to Malaya in the early 1900s to work as
labourers and earth-carriers. Proud of their independence,
the Samsui women made the best of what their own labour
could earn.

Their skills in carting, carrying, scaffolding and mixing
concrete were highly valued and they dominated the
construction field to the 1950s. They could do hard physical
work because their feet were unbound. In the Shanshui
District, the women had to work alongside the men in the
fields, so they were freed from the practice of feet-binding,
a custom prevalent in other areas.

Most Samsui women were either widows or women who
had run away from abusive homes. Nevertheless, all their
lives they worked to send money to their families. Their
remittances were used to meet their families' needs, for the
veneration of ancestors and for fulfillment of ritual vows.

'红头巾'－建筑工人和劳工

另一组意志坚强、独立意识强烈的女性是'红头巾'。她们来自珠江三角洲的三水地区。1900年代，家乡的水灾、粮荒、饥荒迫使她们来到新加坡和马来亚谋生。她们当上了劳工和建筑工人。这些女性为自己的独立自主而自豪，她们尽最大限度地利用自己劳动所赚来的每一分钱。

人们对她们在使用手推车、搬运、搭手架和混水泥方面的技术给予好评。直到1950年代，她们垄断了建筑行业。她们没有缠脚，可干粗活。三水地区一带，女性也像男性一样下田种地，因此并没有像中国其他地方的女性一样缠脚；这使得她们比其他女性更具独立性和行动力。

她们大多数是寡妇，或是因为遭丈夫或家婆虐待而离家的女人。尽管如此，终其一生，她们还是一直把工作赚来的钱寄回家。这些钱被用于一般家用、祭拜祖先和祭祀神灵。

Samsui women at work, Singapore, mid-1900s

voices of the strong and free

It is unquestionably more rewarding to be on your own, making your own money which you can then send home to raise your family... There was no need to depend on anyone or pander to someone else's whims ... instead you are free to do as you wish... Is not this a good thing?

Wong Sau Eng

I prefer to be independent. I don't want to spend my life looking after my in-laws.

Mui Fong

When I first came to Singapore, it was my sisters who took care of my accommodation and helped me to get my first job... These sisters came to Singapore before me, and they were the ones who gave me the idea of coming here. There were times when I missed my family in China very badly. My sisters were the ones who gave me the emotional support. If I had a bad day at work, they were the ones who would console me. We were very close. After all, we were alone in a foreign land.

Ah Moi

Painter Georgette Chen,
Singapore, c. 1920

laundry wives

In China in the old days women thought that people came over to pick gold... Ai! Really! They thought they were coming to Gold Mountain to pick gold! You think they knew they were coming to work in the laundry?

A veteran laundry wife

Chinese laundry wives cooked meals in the back of their shops and took care of their children. They worked with babies strapped to their backs, bending over heaps of clothes. Because of the long hours, their legs were swollen with varicose veins. They rarely stepped out of the shop. One wife recalled that she had left her laundry only three times to attend family functions in the 38 years that she worked there.

Some of these old timers, they work 16 hours a day. They save a few dollars because they have no time to do anything else. The money they picked in their hands, they didn't spend it nowhere, except for their family back in China or Hong Kong.

Andy Eng, manager of Wing Gong Laundry, New York

The remittances of *amahs*, Samsui women and laundry wives helped transform entire villages and districts. Their money paid for roads, schools, clan halls and temples, and also accounted for the high literacy rate among males in the counties. Eventually, girls from enlightened and well-to-do families were also taught to read and write.

坚强与自由之声

凭着自己的劳动赚钱养家，毫无疑问地更有成就感…不用依靠任何人，也不用讨好他人…相反地，你想做什么就做什么…这样不是很好吗?

Wong Sau Eng

我还是比较喜欢独立自主。我不希望花一生照顾婆家。

Mui Fong

我刚到新加坡时，是我的那帮姐妹帮我安排住宿，帮助我找到了第一份工作。这些姐妹都比我先来，就是她们的经历，让我产生了过来的念头。有时候我非常想念在中国的亲人，这时候我的那帮姐妹就成了我的精神支柱。如果我哪天工作不顺心，她们也会安慰我。我们之间关系很亲密。毕竟，我们都是独身一人身处异国他乡。

Ah Moi

洗衣妇

那时的中国女人都以为大家过来是来捡金子的…哎! 真是的! 她们以为她们可以到金山来捡金子! 你以为她们是为了在洗衣店工作才过来的?

一位当年的洗衣妇

她们在洗衣店后面的房间里开饭、照顾孩子、喂奶。她们工作的时候，就把婴儿绑在背上，弯着腰揉洗堆在面前的一大堆衣服。时间一长，她们两只脚上的血管全都肿胀了。

她们很少踏出店门。有位洗衣妇回忆道，她在她丈夫的洗衣店工作了38年，只曾为了参加一些家庭活动而出过三次店门。

有些老手每天工作长达16小时。因为根本没时间做别的事，她们的钱全都省下来了。她们拿到工钱之后，除了把一部分寄回在中国或香港的家里之外，其他都没用到。

Andy Eng，纽约 Wing Gong 洗衣店的经理

包括阿嬷、'红头巾'和洗衣妇在内的妇女寄回家的汇款，还有男人们寄回家的钱，一起改变了他们整个家乡的面貌。这些钱被用来修路、建校、修建祠堂和寺庙，还让家里用上了电。也是由于这些钱，当地县城里的男子也大多可以受到教育。渐渐地，来自比较开通、富裕的家庭里的女孩子也开始可以学习读书写字。

Tenterfield, Australia, c. 1945

education

By the early 1900s, because of better opportunities for
education and developments such as the May 4th Movement,
the voices of Chinese women overseas increasingly began
to be heard. In 1908, Wu Hsueh-hua and Chung Cho-ching
(Yoshiko Watanabe, a Japanese national) founded Kuen
Cheng Girls' School, the first Chinese girls' school in Malaya.
In San Francisco, Sieh King King, an 18-year-old student,
gave an impassioned speech calling for education and
equality for women that was widely reported.

...It is imperative that schools for women be established all over the
country so that all 20 million women in China can acquire reasoning
and practice professions thus allowing them to move forward on a
complementary footing with men...

Chung Sai Yat Poh, 3 November 1902

An orphange in China, late 1800s/early 1900s

In 1903, Mai Zhouyi, a merchant's wife and teacher from
Guangzhou who was educated in a missionary school,
spoke to an audience of 1,500 in the Presbyterian Church
in San Francisco's Chinatown. She had been detained by
the immigration authorities for 40 days in a shed on the
wharf. Besides speaking on education for women, she spoke
passionately for better treatment of immigrants.

...How can it be that they look upon us as animals? As less than cargo?
Do they think we Chinese are not made of flesh and blood? That we don't
have souls? Human beings are supposed to be the superior among all
creatures. Should we allow ourselves to be treated like cargo and dumb
animals? ...If China should become strong one day, I would have a big
stone tablet erected at each trading port to commemorate how America
kept us in captivity. But I would have 'Please enter' carved on it to show the
world that in spite of the unkind treatment accorded us by the Americans,
we Chinese would treat others more generously. Such a response would be
far superior to killing or retaliating in kind.

Chung Sai Yat Poh, 10 June 1903

Three sisters, Vancouver, British Columbia, Canada, c. 1915

Classes, late 1800s/early 1900s

教育

到了**1900**年代早期，由于教育程度的普遍提高和诸如五四运动等事件所带来的社会进步，受过教育的海外华人女性开始吸引人们的注意。**1908**年，吴雪华与钟初清（日本籍）创建了马来亚第一所华人女子学校－群成女子学校。在旧金山，一位叫谢晶晶的十八岁女生为了呼吁关注女性教育和性别平等，做了一次热情洋溢的演讲。旧金山市里的英文报和华文报都报道了她的演讲。

> 在全国各地建立起女子学校是非常重要的。只有这样，中国的两千万女性才可以有机会获得思考和实践的能力，然后让她们可以获得和男子一样的社会地位
>
> 《中西日报》，1902年11月3日

1903年，一位名叫麦周仪的女士在旧金山唐人街的基督教大教堂对着大约**1,500**名听众做了一次演讲。麦周仪是商人的妻子，曾在教会学校受过教育的教师。她入境美国时，被移民官员关在一间港口的小屋里长达**40**天。除了谈到女性受教育的问题之外，她很激动地抗议美国人对待华人移民的态度。

> ...他们怎么可以把我们看作禽兽？比他们的货物都不如？难道他们认为我们中国人就不是血肉和灵魂铸成的？人类应该是万物之长的，难道我们中国人会容忍自己被当成货物和禽兽？...如果有一天中国强大起来了，我希望在每个中国的港口都竖个石碑，上面写上美国人当初是如何禁锢我们中国人的。但我同时也会在上面刻上"请进"两个字，让世人都看看－虽然美国人待我们不好，但我们中国人却有待人的雅量。这种反应要比杀戮和互相报复好得多。
>
> 《中西日报》，1903年6月10日

Kathleen in China, c. 1935

a doctor's story

Kathleen Pih-Chang left her parents and China at the age
of five in 1908. She was adopted by a missionary, her Aunty
Maggie (Margaret Reid), and grew up on a farm in Otago in
the 1910s and 1920s. During her youth, Kathleen refused
to return home to China to marry the man her father had
chosen for her, and she went to study medicine at the
University of Otago where she became the first Chinese
woman in New Zealand to attain a medical degree.

When I started as a house surgeon at Oamaru Hospital, some of the
patients said, 'We are not going to stay here if that Chinese doctor comes'.
But after I did arrive, they didn't leave. At the beginning I was terrified,
just terrified. They got to like me later on...

**She finally returned to China as a doctor and missionary in
the 1930s.**

There were very few women doctors, the villagers liked me and were at
ease with me... I usually saw about 50 patients a day. I was very thorough.
Three days a week we called 'yi-kay' (clinic days) and charged 5 cents for
consultation. The other days we charged 50 cents...

**Between 1935 and 1937, Kathleen studied ophthalmology
at the Royal London Ophthalmic Hospital. She returned
again to China and married Professor Francis Chang, and
they taught at Saint John's University in Shanghai from
the 1930s to 1950.**

I am really glad that I went back to China. As a girl, I did not like being
Chinese at all. The people that I admired were the Scots. I accept that I am
Chinese now, but I was very sensitive about it when I was young. Going
back to work in China in the 1930s was really good for me, otherwise I
would always have felt so sorry for myself for being born Chinese. Only
after working in China did I find my Chinese identity.

医生

1908年，五岁的Kathleen Pih-Chang离开了亲生父母，离开了中国，移民到纽西兰。身为传教士的'Maggie阿姨'（Margaret Reid）收养了她，她在奥达哥的农场度过了1910年代和1920年代。

年轻时的Kathleen不愿意回中国嫁给她父亲为她挑选好的男人。她选择了进入奥达哥大学读医学，并成为了纽西兰第一个获得医学学位的华人女性。

> 我开始在欧阿马如医院住院部当外科医生时，有些病人说：'如果那中国女医生来这里的话，我们可不会留下来'。但后来我去到医院，他们也没真的走掉。一开始我很害怕，不知为什么就是很害怕。后来，他们渐渐开始喜欢我了…

Kathleen at home

1930年代，她终于以医生和传教士的身份回到中国。

> 女医生并不多，村民们都很喜欢我，对我很和善…我一天通常替大约50个病人看病。我很细心地做事。一个星期里有三天是我们的'医期'，看病只收5分钱。其他时候我们的收费是5角钱…

1935年到1937年，Kathleen到伦敦眼科医院学眼科治疗。她之后又回到中国，嫁给Francis Chang教授。他们1930年代到1950年代期间在上海的圣约翰大学教书。

> 我很庆幸那时回了中国。我年轻时一点也不喜欢当中国人。我欣赏的是苏格兰人。现在我接受我是个中国人的事实了，但我年轻时对这问题很敏感。1930年代时回到中国对我来说是件大好事，否则我会永远抱怨自己是中国人。就是在中国工作了一段时间之后，我才认同自己的确是中国人。

Kathleen with her adopted sister in Otago, New Zealand

新加坡:向往南洋

汤姆斯·史丹福·莱佛士1819年在新加坡建立起贸易口岸之后，大量华人移民来到了新加坡，开辟当地的胡椒和甘密种植业。华商、苦力与卖艺人为新加坡的发展提供了资金和劳动力。

1900年代初期，华人掌控了橡胶贸易和银行业，尤其是福建人和潮州人。他们创立了银行，打破了欧洲人对金融市场的垄断。后来，李光前成功合并了当地的三家华人银行，成立了如今的华侨银行。

华商有行善的传统，慷慨地向学校和其他公益组织捐赠献款。'巴巴'（男性土生华人的称呼）商人兼太平绅士陈笃生，建立了一所后来以他名字命名的穷人医院。其他企业家，如颜永成、林文庆医生和陈嘉庚，资助建立了当地的华文学校或英文学校。1923年，具有英国律师背景的新加坡立法会成员宋旺相爵士，撰写了大作《新加坡华人百年史》。

对新加坡华人来说，日本入侵中国、入侵占领马来亚和新加坡那段时期是见证数千人丧命的痛苦日子。自1963年独立之后，新加坡在李光耀的领导下，实行多元种族政策。

> 我那九十四岁的祖母过世了。
> 她生于那个疆域广大、历史渊长的国家的土地上，
> 在那里不需要摇摆不定的指南针，
> 在那里宏大的地图让人浮想。
> 为何她要离开那个有着漫长的过去与未来的地方？
> 而来到这片没有过去、只有不确实的未来的土地上？
> 因为这个年轻女子的故事，
> 和她那小小的、不知未来的穿海越洋，
> 开启了我的故事的篇章。
>
> Keith Tan,《旅程》

Singapore: Nanyang Bound

After Stamford Raffles founded a trading settlement in Singapore in 1819, Chinese immigrants arrived in large numbers and pioneered the cultivation of gambier and pepper. Chinese merchants, coolies and artisans provided the capital and labour that contributed to the development of colonial Singapore.

In the early 1900s, the Chinese, especially the Hokkiens and Teochews, dominated the rubber trade and banking. They founded banks and broke the European monopoly on financial services. Later, three Chinese banks merged to form the modern Overseas Chinese Banking Corporation under Lee Kong Chian.

Chinese merchants had a tradition of philanthropy and gave generously to schools and other public institutions. Baba merchant Tan Tock Seng, a Justice of the Peace, founded the paupers' hospital that was later named for him. Other entrepreneurs like Gan Eng Seng, Dr Lim Boon Keng and Tan Kah Kee founded Chinese and English schools. In 1923, Sir Song Ong Siang, a British-trained lawyer and member of the Legislative Council, published his massive volume *One Hundred Years' History of the Chinese in Singapore*.

For the Singaporean Chinese community, the Japanese invasion of China and the Japanese Occupation of Malaya were painful years that saw the death of thousands. Since independence in 1963, Singapore has pursued a policy of multiculturalism under the stewardship of Lee Kuan Yew.

My grandmother died when she was ninety-four.
Born to a world of fixed geographies, unchanging histories, using
Stable compasses and proud maps that spoke only to themselves.
Why did she abandon her history-fixed future
To enter a world with no history, only an unknown future?
My history begins in the story of this young woman
And of her small uncertain steps across a crowded ocean.

Keith Tan, *Journeys*

纽西兰:新定义

从1865年来到纽西兰的金矿工人，到1900年代初期的华人洗衣铺老板、水果商和菜农，华人在纽西兰已有了超过130年的历史。大多数华人金矿工人后来回了中国，但有些留了下来，在威灵顿这样的城市中心定居。少数移民，如定居丹尼丁的徐肇开和威灵顿的郭期颐，成了富商；张朝，一位极具企业精神的前金矿工人，创办了纽西兰最早的牛油工厂之一。但这些只是极少数的特例。总的来说，纽西兰华人被排斥于其主流社会之外。

二战之后，纽西兰政府批准了少量的入境准证给当地土生及移民华人的家人。纽西兰华人人数很少；1951年的人口调查显示仅有约五千人，但他们享有不错的生活水准。

> 我这一代，出生于1960年代后期，所受的教育和上一代完全不同。虽然我也是在家里的水果店长大的...我从来不须辛苦工作。我也不是以严格的传统方式带大的。除了有时遇到种族歧视的情况之外，总的来说我一直过的很不错。
> 最值得注意的可能是我这一代所受的'纽西兰化'教育。我们在家中常用的语言是英语。所以尽管我们每个星期都上广东课，我们大多数人还是只会讲一点点或完全不会讲广东话...

1996年，华人人口占了纽西兰总人口的2%。其中超过75%的华人是在当地出生的；许多是华人和欧洲人、毛利人或萨摩亚人的混血儿。现代的纽西兰华裔，如名作家柯斯顿·王、电影制片人哈利·王和唐纳德·吴等，正在为'纽西兰华裔'创立着新定义。

New Zealand: New Identities

From the goldminers who arrived in New Zealand in 1865 to the laundry owners, fruiterers and market gardeners of the early 1900s, the Chinese have been part of New Zealand for over 130 years. Although most of the Chinese goldminers returned to China, some remained in urban centres like Wellington. A few immigrants like Sew Hoy in Dunedin and William Kwok in Wellington became wealthy merchants, and an enterprising former goldminer, Chew Chong, started one of the earliest butter factories in New Zealand. They were the exceptions, however. By and large, Chinese New Zealanders were excluded from mainstream society.

After World War II, the government allowed a limited number of entry permits for families of New Zealand-born Chinese and naturalised Chinese. The Chinese community was small, numbering about 5,000 in the 1951 census, but it enjoyed a relatively modest standard of living.

...My own generation, those born in the later 1960s, had a very different upbringing. Although I grew up in the family fruit shop... I never had to work hard. Nor was I brought up in a strictly traditional fashion. Life, apart from the occasional experience of racism, was good.

 It is perhaps the very 'New Zealandness' of my generation's upbringing which is notable. English was the common language spoken at home, with the result that most of my peers speak little or no Cantonese, despite being packed off to weekly Cantonese classes...

Kirsten Wong

In 1996, the Chinese formed 2% of New Zealand's population. More than 75% of these were local-born, and many are of European-Chinese, Maori-Chinese or Samoan-Chinese parentage. Today, Chinese New Zealanders like writer Kirsten Wong and filmmakers Harry Wong and Donald Ng are redefining what it means to be a Chinese New Zealander.

Bonds

The Chinese who sojourned overseas maintained bonds with their past and each other through letters, clan associations, and the passing down of stories, traditions and values.

旅居海外的
华人，通过
信件、会馆
和故事、传
统与价值观
的传递，跟
过去与彼此
保持联系。

Family portrait, Singapore, c. 1920

Vancouver, British Columbia, Canada, c. 1905

letters

Lack of funds and the exclusion laws in America, Canada
and Australia forced thousands of Chinese men overseas
to live as bachelors, and their wives in China as virtual
widows. The letters of these women, written with the help
of professional letter-writers, provide a glimpse of their
feelings as they reminded their loved ones of their duties.

I hear that you, my son, are acting the prodigal... For many months there
has arrived no letter or money. My supplies are exhausted. I am old; too
infirm to work... Hereafter, my son, change your course; be industrious
and frugal, and remit to me your earnings; and within the year let me
welcome home both your father and yourself.

A mother to her son

Letter writers in Chinatown, together with stores like the
Kam Wah Chung Company in Oregon and herbal shops such
as Eu Yang Sang in Malaya helped the Chinese overseas to
remit money, and to send letters and photographs.

...we two are separated by mountain and ocean... I always pray to God to
bless you to enable you to make a good chance [have good luck] so that you
can return with your fortune to your home... I sincerely hope you... do not
squander your valuable time in the opium and prostitute places...

A wife to her husband

Extended family portrait, Singapore, early 1900s

Couple, Vancouver, British Columbia, Canada, c. 1939

Letter-writer and customer, Singapore, mid-1900s

信件

在美国、澳洲和加拿大，成千上万个海外华人男子由于缺乏经费，再加上当地限制华人入境的移民法律，被迫过着独身生活。他们留在中国的妻子也像是守起了活寡。女性们托写信佬写的信，让我们看到她们规劝男人们要有责任心时的心态。

儿子、听说你现在放荡...几个月来，从没收到过你的一封信或一分钱。我的生活必需品已经快光了。我年纪也大了，没有力气干活...儿子，希望你从此改过，勤劳节俭，把赚到的钱寄回给我；希望一年内可以迎接你们父子俩归来。

母亲寄儿子之信

唐人街帮人写信念信的这些写信佬、公司（如美国奥勒冈州的金华忠公司）和中药行（如在马来亚的余仁生药店），都帮助了海外华人汇钱、写信、寄照片回家。

我们之间山海相隔。我一直祈求上天保佑你财运亨通，赶快赚到钱就回家。我真的不希望你把宝贵的时间浪费在烟花之地...

妻子寄丈夫之信

Sixth Annual Management Committee, Hakka Association, Singapore, mid-1900s

associations

The overseas Chinese established *huiguan* (clan or native associations) wherever they sojourned in adequate numbers. These associations provided people of the same surname, district or dialect group with a place to stay, socialise and get financial assistance.

[These mutual aid associations were] part of the collective adaptation of ethnic Chinese... They kept migrants informed of developments in their places of origin ... provided members with a measure of assistance and protection from discrimination by non-Chinese and against competition from rival Chinese groups.

Wing Chung Ng, Canada

Mutual aid associations could be found in Chinatowns around the world. One of the earliest in Canada was the Chinese Benevolent Association, which was founded in Victoria, British Columbia, in 1884. Such groups in North America led the protest against exclusionist immigration policies. In Malaya, associations helped maintain ties between members of the community, and served their economic and social needs. The common ones were the Guangdong Association, the Fujian Association, the Teochew Association and the Hakka Association.

The secret societies and triads like the Ghee Hin and the Hai
San in nineteenth century Malaya also helped the Chinese,
particularly the tin miners, to maintain links with the
community. These were not secretive or anti-government
groups until they were banned in 1890 when the British
considered their rivalries disruptive of trade and peace. In
New Zealand, associations were founded to help the gold
miners keep in touch with their native villages. The Poon
Fah Association, founded in New Zealand in 1869, was a
benevolent association that served the men from the Punyu
and Fa counties. There were clan associations as well in
the Caribbean Islands, where the Chinese population was
around 10,000 or less on each island. In Trinidad were the
Taishan, Xinhui, Sanyi and Zhongshan associations, with
similar groups in Cuba. In Jamaica, there was the Chinese
Benevolent Association, in Guyana the Chinese Association,
and in Surinam, the Guanyi Tang Sheng.

Hakka Association, Singapore, mid-1900s

Vancouver, British Columbia, Canada, c. 1910

会馆

海外华人聚居的地方，只要人数够多，都会设立会馆。这些会馆为同族、同乡或同籍贯的人提供了寄宿、来往、求助的地方。

> （这些互助会）是华人适应他乡的一部分。会馆告诉海外华人们家乡的发展情况，给会员们提供经援帮助，对抗其他族群对华人的歧视，并与对立的华人团体相互竞争。
>
> **Wing Chung Ng**，加拿大

在世界各国的唐人街都找得到互助会馆。在加拿大最早创立的互助会馆之一是中华仁慈会馆，于1884年在维多利亚成立。在加拿大和美国的华人会馆领导了反对排华的移民法律的运动。在马来亚的会馆帮助维系会员之间的联络，满足他们在经济上与社会交往方面的需求。各地比较普遍的会馆包括了广东会馆、福建会馆、潮州会馆和客家会馆。

> 直到政府设立华人保护区之前，英国人一直没有直接干涉华人的事务。殖民地当局通过当地华人上层人士控制、管理华人。这些上层人士包括了当地的知名华人和各个帮派头目。这些人通常在众多家族、庙宇、商铺和各地方会馆担当要职。
>
> 《海外华人百科全书》

19世纪在马来亚所谓的私会党，如义兴党和海山党，也帮了华人，特别是锡矿工人，保持与社会的联系。这些党派其实并不是秘密或反政府组织，但到了1890年，英国殖民政府觉得这些党派彼此之间的敌对关系扰乱了商业活动和当地治安，因而取缔了它们。

在纽西兰，为了方便华人金矿工人和家乡保持联系，于是成立了会馆。番花会馆（昌善堂）于1869年在纽西兰成立。这是来自番禺、花县的人组织的慈善机构。在加勒比海群岛，华人的人数大概是每岛一万个人或不到；那里也有会馆。在特里尼达有台山、新会、三义和中山会馆。在古巴也有类似的会馆。在牙买加有中华会馆。圭亚那也有中华会馆，而在苏里南有广义堂。

团结就是力量

1907年，南非华人劳工超过六万名。广东人把南非约翰斯堡的广东会馆称为光福堂，为来自广东的华人服务。1900年代中期，当时在约翰斯堡当律师的印度'圣雄'甘地描述广东会馆，以表支持：

> 这里没有可以让华人寄宿的地方，因此他们开办了一个广东会馆，是一个可见客、寄宿、也是图书馆的场所。他们长期租下了一片土地，建了平房。那里的屋子很干净，空间也不小，里里外外看来都像个豪华的欧洲俱乐部。里面有许多具有不同功能的房间：画室、餐厅、会议室、委员会专用房间和秘书室，以及图书馆。他们严格按照各个房间的功能使用这些房间。屋子里还有其他房间，会馆的人就把它们当成客房出租和提供寄宿。这个地方很豪华、很干净，就连到访本地的华人名流绅士都在这里寄宿。会馆的入会费是每人5英镑，每个会员再按照自己职业的不同每年缴纳不同数目的年费。这个会馆现在大概有150个会员，他们每个星期天都有聚会，游乐消遣。会员平时也可以使用会馆的设施。

美国、加拿大、澳洲和纽西兰早期时候的会馆现在都消失了。那些在东南亚的会馆则随着时代改变了。他们许多被超越了籍贯界限的中华总商会和中华会馆之类的组织取代了。

Mahatma Gandhi (second from left) with members of the Cantonese Association, Johannesburg, South Africa, early 1900s

Students in America, c. 1881

strength in unity

By 1907, there were more than 60,000 Chinese workers in South Africa. In Johannesburg, the Cantonese Club was known as the Kwong Hok Tong and catered to the Chinese from Guangdong. In the mid-1900s, Mohandas Karamchand Gandhi, who was then a lawyer in Johannesburg, wrote in support of the club:

Since the Chinese have no facilities for lodging, they have started a Cantonese Club which serves as a meeting place, a lodge and also as a library. They have acquired for the Club land on a long lease and have built on it a pucca one-storeyed building. There they all live in great cleanliness and do not stint themselves in the matter of living space, and seen within and from outside, it would look like some good European club. They have in it separate rooms marked drawing, dining, meeting, committee room and the Secretary's room, and the library, and do not use any room except for the purpose for which it is intended. Other rooms adjoining these are let out as bedrooms. It is such a fine and clean place that any Chinese gentleman visiting the town can be put up there. The entrance fee is five pounds, and the annual subscription varies according to the members' profession. The Club has about 150 members who meet every Sunday and amuse themselves with games. The members can avail themselves of Club facilities on week-days also.

Many of the early clan associations died out in America, Canada, Australia and New Zealand. Those in Southeast Asia redefined themselves to fit modern conditions. Many were replaced by organisations such as the Chinese Chambers of Commerce and *zhonghua hui* (Chinese associations) that cut across dialect groups.

Storyteller and audience by the Singapore River, mid-1900s

Market gardener and friend,
Wagga Wagga, Australia, c. 1959

telling stories

There were itinerant storytellers in many Chinatowns, and
one way of keeping in touch was through storytelling at the
clan association.

On Sundays, my father and I (I'm the oldest) used to go over to there [Ket
Hing Society] and then there was a gambling joint there. All the men folks
would be gambling. And they would all be listening to the storytellers.
They would have a couple of people who had communication with China.
This man would sit down and everybody would gather around him, and he
would be telling stories, especially of the history of China, of Confucius,
and the Taoist way of life.

A Chinese who grew up in Hawaii in the early 1900s

Imagine it is evening. The shops are closed for the night.
Many people, including children, gather around a storyteller
on the sidewalk. He lights an oil lamp and a joss stick, and
plays a few notes on his zither. More people crowd around
or sit on low wooden stools. He sings a song and begins to
unravel an absorbing tale of a great hero. Now and then he
plays a few notes on his Chinese zither or uses a stick to
hit a piece of bamboo for a sound effect. When the joss stick
burns out, the storyteller stops. His audience digs into their
pockets. They throw a few coins into his box. When everyone
has done so, the storyteller lights another joss stick and
continues his tale.

讲故事

许多唐人街里都找得到说书人，而华人之间保持联系的一个好方法
就是在公司里听故事、讲故事。

每个星期天，父亲就带我（我是最大的孩子）去那里（洼兴会）。那时有个赌场。大
家有时会赌钱，有时也会听人讲故事。他们有些跟中国有联络，这人会坐下来，大家
都在他身边围成一团。这人就开始讲故事，尤其是关于中国历史、儒家学说、道家的
养生之道等的故事。

1900年代早期在夏威夷长大的华人

试想一个傍晚，所有商店已经关门。许多人，包括很多小孩子，围
着坐在街边的说书人。他点一盏油灯和一支香。更多人围过来，有
些坐在木矮凳上。他先唱首小曲，然后开始讲述精彩的武侠故事。
他不时弹几下琴，或用木枝敲一下竹块，制造声响效果。一支香烛
烧完，他就停下来，听众们便从口袋里掏钱丢进说书人的盒子里。
大家都给了钱后，说书人就再点上一支香，继续讲下去。

消息

海外华人特别重视教育与文化。不论到那里居住，都会出版报纸，
帮助海外华人保持与中国的联系。通过报章、杂志，甚至墙壁、店
面贴的海报，许多海外华人社会间接性地参与了中国事务。

这些报章有时非常严厉地批评西方政府的移民法律。《中西日报》
是Ng Poon Chew医生1904年在旧金山创立的，它大胆地表达了美
国华裔的心声。

所有华人，不论是商人、官员、教师、学生或游客，在美国都被贬低至狗的身份。这
些'狗'一定要有挂'牌子'（居留准证），以代表他们的合法身份，才能出门。要
不然，他们就会像没有登记、没有主人的狗一般，被捉送进居留营。

《中西日报》1906年4月2日

Storybook illustration, Singapore, early 1900s

the news

Reading the news, America

Education and culture were highly valued by the overseas Chinese. Wherever they settled, they published newspapers that kept them in touch with each other. Through their newspapers, magazines and even posters pasted on walls and shopfronts, many overseas Chinese communities participated (albeit vicariously) in the affairs of China. At times, these newspapers were also critical of the immigration laws of western governments. The *Chung Sai Yat Poh* was founded by Dr Ng Poon Chew in San Francisco in 1904. Through it, he articulated the views of the Chinese in America.

...all Chinese whether they are merchants or officials, teachers, students or tourists, are reduced to the status of dogs in America. The dogs must have with them necklaces [certificates of residence] which attest to their legal status before they are allowed to go out. Otherwise they would be arrested as unregistered, unowned dogs and would be herded into a detention camp.

Chung Sai Yat Poh, 2 April 1906

Wallfront bulletins, America, late 1800s/early 1900s

173

Classroom, America, early 1900s

school

The first generation of Chinese settlers were very conscious of being different from the non-Chinese majority. They set up Chinese schools and insisted that their children learnt the culture of the old country. Some families even forbade their children from speaking English at home, and insisted that they attend special classes to study Mandarin, the *San Zhi Jing* (*Three-Character Primer*) and calligraphy.

My Chinese school career began when I was five years old... The school was on Grant Avenue. We went to Chinese school immediately after American school which was about 4 or 5 p.m. and stayed there till 7 or 8 p.m.

Edward LC, San Francisco, early 1900s

...we never became proficient in reading or writing Chinese—probably because we never thought of ourselves as needing Chinese. After all, weren't we Americans?

Thomas W Chinn, who founded the *Chinese Digest* in 1935

In Southeast Asia from the 1850s to the early 1900s, many small schools were established by impoverished teachers and scholars, while bigger schools were richly funded by entrepreneurs. In 1849, a wealthy philanthropist, Tan Kim Seng, founded Chong Wen Ge, the first Chinese language school in Singapore, and in 1886, a Straits-born Chinese, Gan Eng Seng, founded the Anglo-Chinese Free School.

Besides reading Chinese books, younger generations of overseas Chinese learnt about the literature, history and culture of China through books written in other languages. The Straits Chinese in Malaya used a written language based on Romanised Malay. By the 1890s, many Baba Malay translations of popular Chinese classics had been published by Chan Kim Boon, a writer who wrote under the pen name of Batu Gantung. Chan was born in Penang in 1851 and his publications included translations of *Sam Kok* (*The Three Kingdoms*), *Song Kang* (*Water Margin*) and *Chrita Seh Yew* (*Journey to the West*).

Fiction Monthly,
Singapore, mid-1900s;
Children's Songs,
Singapore, c. 1947

Students, Jakarta, Indonesia, c. 1900

Classroom, Italy, late 1900s

The Kwok siblings, New Zealand, early 1900s

上学

第一代海外华人移民意识到自己和占多数的非华人不同。他们设立华人学校，坚持让下一代学故国文化。有些家庭甚至不准孩子在家里讲英语，坚持让他们上特别课程，读《三字经》、学书法。

我的华文学校生涯在我五岁那年开始学校在格兰特街。我们上完美国学校的课程，大概是四五点钟了，然后马上赶到华文学校上课，直到七八点。

1900年代住在旧金山的Edward LC

我们从没精通读写华文的能力－大概是因为我们从没想到过我们会需要用到华语。我们难道不是美国人吗?

1935年创办 *Chinese Digest* 的 Thomas W Chin

从1850年代中期到1900年代初，在东南亚出现了许多由不怎么有钱的教师、学者开办的小型学校，而较大型的学府由富家大力支持。1849年，富裕的慈善家陈金声创办了新加坡第一间华文学校－崇文阁。1886年，马六甲出生的华人颜永成创立了英华义学。

除了阅读华文书籍，年轻一代的海外华人通过其他语言写的书本学习中国文学、历史与文化。马来亚的海峡华人使用一种罗马化的马来拼音文字。到了1890年代，一位叫陈金文，笔名Batu Gantung 的作者用'巴巴'马来文出版了许多中国名著。他于1851年在槟城出生，出版了包括《三国》、《水浒》和《西游记》在内的中国名著翻译版本。

Zhong Chuan Primary School, China, c. 2002

School portrait, Dunedin, New Zealand, c. 1947

Students with class mascot, sports day at Napier Girls High School, New Zealand, c. 1948

马来西亚:新旧移民

最早来到马来西亚的华人移民是于15世纪随着郑和船队到达马六甲的商人。他们在马来亚定居下来,娶了当地人作妻子。他们的后代-'巴巴'(土生华人)-构成了现代马来西亚华人社会的一小部分。

其他大部分的华人移民则是'新客',他们是于19世纪时来到属于英国殖民地的马来亚的华人及其后代。这些华人移民中大多数是契约劳工,听从同族的领袖或劳工代办的指挥。他们散居到了马来亚、沙巴和砂劳越等地,主要是福建人、广东人、客家人、潮州人、福州人和兴化人。19世纪末,马来亚许多锡矿的控制权被掌握在各个华人移民团体的手中。势力最大的两个团体是'义兴'(由广东人组成)和'海山'(由客家人组成)。这些团体是按照其族群和所讲的方言组成的,处于由马来苏丹和英国人所指定的'甲必丹'(意为'华人首领')的领导之下。华人领袖们负责维持着华人社群里的法律和秩序。其中一个是叶亚莱,吉隆坡是由他领导建设起来的。

20世纪初期,富有的华人企业家为这个国家注入了开办贸易和种植业所需的劳动力和资金。他们也创办了华文学校,保留中国的传统教育和文化。如今,马来西亚华裔都讲马来语,而且他们大多数人也会华语和英语。在马来西亚的各个阶层之中都有华人的身影。其中有成功的企业家,也有在法律、医药、科技和媒体等各个领域里工作的专业人士。

Malaysia: Old and New Sojourners

The earliest Chinese immigrants came to Malaya to trade at the time of Zheng He, who visited Malacca in the fifteenth century. They settled there and married local women. Their descendants, the Babas or Straits Chinese, form a unique part of the Malaysian Chinese population today.

Thousands of Chinese immigrants, the *sinkhehs* ('new sojourners') came during the period of British colonial rule in the nineteenth century. Most were indentured labourers beholden to clan leaders and labour brokers. They were Hokkien, Cantonese, Hakka, Teochew, Fuzhou and Henghua who came to Malaya, Sabah and Sarawak. In the late nineteenth century, groups of Chinese immigrants fought for control of the tin mining areas in Malaya. The two most prominent groups were the Ghee Hin and the Hai San, two associations organised by clan and dialect under the leadership of *kapitan Cina* (Chinese captains) like Yap Ah Loy, the founder of Kuala Lumpur. *Kapitan cina* were prominent men appointed by the Malay kings and the British to maintain law and order within the Chinese community.

In the early twentieth century, Chinese entrepreneurs brought in the necessary labour and capital to fuel the pioneering work in opening up the country for trade and plantation agriculture. They also founded Chinese schools which sought to preserve Chinese culture. Today, all Malaysian Chinese study the Malay language and the majority learn Mandarin and English as well. Malaysian Chinese work in every level of society as entrepreneurs and professionals in law, medicine, technology and the media.

泰国：长远历史

1766年缅甸军队围攻当时的泰国首都阿瑜陀，华人居民伸出援手保卫首都，从19世纪起定居泰国。

> 湄南河流域的人口一半以上是华人，几乎没人是一点华人血统都没有的。这些华人既不是农奴，也不是奴隶，可在泰国国土上自由往来
>
> 英国探险家Holt S Hallet 于1890年

19世纪时，来自广东和福建的华人移民占大部分。许多显赫的华人家族，如许氏、黉利、蓝三等，与泰国王室和上流阶层有着各种形式的通婚和商业关系。他们在泰国建立起庞大的商业组织，经营范围包括碾米、保险和银行业。许泗漳原本是一个来自福建的劳工，凭着锡矿开采和税收承包积攒了财富。他担任税吏十分成功，因此被泰国国王封为府尹。许氏家族的成员在泰国是成功的企业家和重要的政治领袖。

20世纪上半段，泰国民族主义兴起，促使政府采取一些措施抑制华人对泰国经济的支配。1913年，泰国通过了泰国国籍法，规定任何泰国人所生的子女，不论其出生地，都是泰国公民。从1900年代至1940年代，政府通过了一系列措施限制华人的经济、教育活动和文化诉求。

二战后，许多泰国华人成为了泰国公民。多年以来，他们为自己取了泰国名字。如今，泰国华人已深深植根于泰国社会的各阶层。许多泰国华人家族名声显赫，如创办盘谷银行的陈氏家族，以及创办泰国最大企业之一的正大集团的谢氏家族。

> （我母亲）在泰国住了50年比许多土生泰国人更爱泰国。她病重时，我们问她要不要回中国。她说泰国才是她的家，她不愿离开。
>
> 林明达，泰华混血儿，一位报刊出版人

Thailand: A New Home

Chinese settlers helped defend Ayudhya during the Burmese siege of the city in 1766, and have lived in Thailand since the nineteenth century.

Half the population of the Meh Nam Delta is Chinese, and very few of the people are without some trace of Chinese blood in them. The Chinese are neither serfs nor slaves, and can go as they will throughout the country...

British traveller Holt S Hallet, 1890

In the nineteenth century, the majority of Chinese immigrants were from Guangdong and Fujian provinces. Families like the Khaws, the Wanglees and the Lamsams had marriage and business links to Thai royalty and the upper echelons of society. These families established a network of enterprises ranging from rice milling to insurance and banking. Khaw Soo Cheang was a Hokkien labourer who built a fortune based on a tin tax farm. He was so successful in collecting revenue for the crown that he was appointed governor, and his family played an important role as entrepreneurs and civic leaders.

Rising nationalism during the early twentieth century gave rise to measures to curb the economic dominance of the Chinese. The 1913 Thai Nationality Law stated that all persons born to a Thai parent anywhere was a Thai citizen, and from the 1900s to 1940s, measures to curtail the Chinese economic activity, education and cultural expression were implemented.

The post-war period saw many Chinese become naturalised Thai citizens, and over the years, they have assumed Thai names. Today, Thai-Chinese are assimilated into all levels of society. Prominent Sino-Thai families include the Sophonpanich family, founders of Bangkok Bank, and the Chearavanont family, founders of Charoen Pokphand, one of the largest Thai conglomerates.

Living 50 years under royal aegis... loving Thailand more than some native Thais. When [my mother] was very ill, we asked her whether she wanted to visit mainland China. She said that Thailand was her home and she did not want to leave the country.

Sondhi Limthongkul, a newspaper publisher of Thai-Chinese ancestry

Food

A common Chinese saying states that
'Eating is *fu* (good fortune)'. How wonderful
it is to eat! Those who have experienced hunger
will appreciate the gift of food.
When a Chinese person meets another,
he or she invariably asks, 'Have you eaten?'
This courteous enquiry is the equivalent of the
Western greeting, 'How are you?'

俗语说：'能吃是
福'。有得吃是件
多美好的事！凡是
挨过饿的，都会感
受到：有东西吃，
是种福气。华人碰
面时，会问对方：
'吃饱了没？'这
和西方人的'你好
吗？'一样，是礼
貌的问候。

Street vendor, Chinatown, America, early 1900s

Singapore, late 1800s/early 1900s

eating and good fortune

...How a Chinese spirit glows over a good feast! How apt is he to cry out
that life is beautiful when his stomach and his intestines are well-filled!

Lin Yutang, *The Importance of Living*

Chinese sojourners were great cooks. Wherever they went,
they brought snacks and sweets that were sold and eaten
at markets, temples, gardens and along sidewalks. The
appreciation of food is part of the Chinese heritage, and was
one of the most important links that the Chinese overseas
had with China. *Towkays* and coolies alike brought their
food to the shores of the new lands, and in any sizeable
overseas Chinese community, there was bound to be a
teahouse or a restaurant for *dim sum* or *yum cha*.

Fishmonger, America, early 1900s

Fruit stall, Honolulu, late 1800s/early 1900s

吃与福

…看着盛莚的中国人，整个灵魂都在雀跃吧！用餐后、心满意足之时，他是多么想大声喊道："生命真美好！"

林语堂，*The Importance of Living*

所有华人移民都很会做吃的。无论到那里－市场、寺庙、公园、路上，他们经常都会带上零食和甜点。饮食欣赏是华人传统文化的一部分，是海外华人和中国最重要的联系之一。'头家'（老板）和苦力们将他们故乡的食物引进了新的居住地；在海外，只要有华人聚居，就一定能找到供应茶点的茶楼和餐馆。

Camp cooks, America, late 1800s/early 1900s

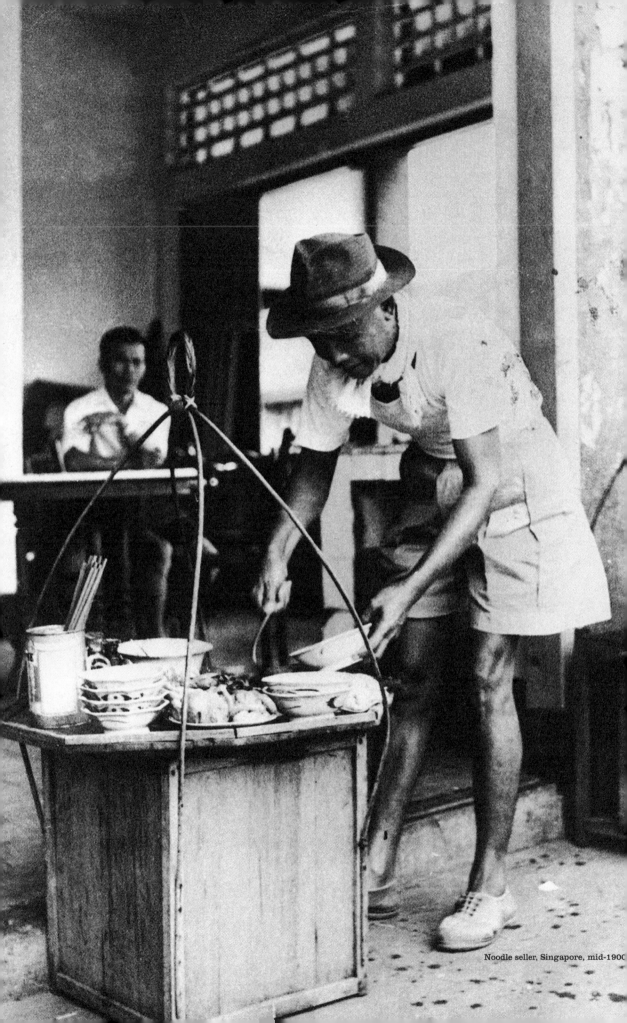

Noodle seller, Singapore, mid-1900

Night hawker, Singapore, mid-1900s

great tastes

Sun Yun Wo, a popular Chinese teahouse in Honolulu's Chinatown, was established in 1892. What a guest saw one day at Sun Yun Wo in the 1930s could have been a scene from any Chinatown teahouse in the world.

Day after day, Chinese businessmen and intellectuals filled the large room on the second floor of this large establishment for dim sum—second breakfast or early lunch. The tables were bare, their crosspieces well worn by the feet that had been propped up on them. Chinese bamboo stools still lined the walls for use at banquets, but common chairs had replaced them at the tables laid with chopsticks and Chinese crockery. Each guest prepared his own tea by pouring boiling-hot water into a bowl containing tea leaves; there were no teapots. Over the plates of such foods as *siu mai*, *kau tse*, *ma tai shu*, *dau sa bau* and over bowls of tea, groups of Chinese conversed on many subjects. In one corner a group might be discussing the increase of freight rates on goods from China or the troubles of dealing with customs officials.

In another corner a group of young newspapermen might be discussing the recent turns in the political affairs of China or an editorial in the last issue of the Sun Chung Kwock Bo. At one table, a group of Chinese language schoolteachers might be lamenting the lack of interest shown by their students in mastering Chinese. At another table, an elderly, poorly clad Chinese man might be listening intently while a young man read to him and explained a letter from China, or translated a letter written in English by a son attending college on the US mainland. Here was laughter and heated argument, and above the bustle and talk, the waiters could be heard sending their orders down the dumbwaiter to the kitchen below. In earlier years no women would have been seen in such a place of eating and leisurely conversation, but by the thirties one occasionally saw a local-born Chinese girl there, perhaps bringing some Caucasian friends seeking the atmosphere of the old Chinatown.

Clarence E Glick, *Sojourners and Settlers: Chinese Migrants in Hawaii*

美味小食

Sun Yun Wo是一间1892年设立于火奴鲁鲁唐人街的著名华人茶楼。客人1930年代在Sun Yun Wo所看到的情景，反映了当时世界各地唐人街的情形：

这间茶楼第二层大厅里每天都坐满了华商和读书人，吃着茶点－这是华人的第二份早餐，又或是他们提前的午餐。桌子上并没有什么特别的装饰，横木也因为人们经常把脚垫在上面而磨损了。中国式的竹凳仍然放在墙边，供席宴需要时使用；但那些放着筷子、碗碟的桌子旁边的竹凳被普通椅子取代了。这里没有茶壶，客人得自己动手把开水倒入已经放好了茶叶的碗里、各自沏茶来喝。华人在这里各自结群，讨论着自己关心的话题，一边吃着烧卖、饺子、马蹄酥、豆沙包，一边饮茶。一个角落里，一群人可能正在讨论从中国进口货物的运费的提高，或是和海关官员们打交道的困难。

另一个角落里，几个年轻记者可能正在讨论中国最近政治事件的发展，或是《新中国报》最新一期的专栏内容。几个华文教师可能正在埋怨学生们欠缺学习华文的兴趣。另一桌，穿着简单的华人老翁可能正在专注地听一个年轻男子帮他解读从中国的来信，或是翻译儿子从美国大学写来的英文信。这里有欢笑有争论；而在喧闹中听得到升降机的声音。茶楼伙计们用它把点菜单送到楼下的厨房去。一开始时，这种可以用餐、畅谈的地方并没有女子出现；但到了1930年代，就偶尔可以见到当地土生的华人女子出入其中，有时还带来一些想在唐人街寻找怀旧气氛的洋人朋友。

Clarence E Glick, *Sojourners and Settlers: Chinese Migrants in Hawaii*

Cooks at work, WK Restaurant, Vancouver, British Columbia, Canada, c. 1947

Tea seller, Thailand, late 1800s

tea

What is Chinese dining without tea? The eighth century
writer Lu Yu was the first to write about tea in his classic,
Cha Ching (*The Tea Chronicle*). It was said that true
connoisseurs of tea could tell whether a cup of tea was
brewed with water from a river or a well, and if the water
was from a river, whether it came from the banks or the
turbulent midstream.

Tea was drunk by all classes of Chinese society, from the
scholar-mandarins to the humble coolies. Descendants
of the Chinese labourers who worked on the American
transcontinental railroad recounted how their great-
grandfathers had it written in their contracts that they
would be given hot, boiled tea every day. The Chinese cooks
used to carry pots of tea to the tracks at the appointed hours,
and it is likely that tea saved many Chinese railroad builders
from the illnesses that befell their Western compatriots who
drank unboiled river water.

茶

吃中国餐怎可没有茶来配？中国的陆羽在8世纪时撰写了第一本专门关于茶的书－《茶经》。据说，以前的品茶专家们可以辨别出一杯茶水是用河水还是井水泡制的，而若是河水，是从河边还是从河中央取来的。

从读书人到卑微的苦力，社会各个阶层的华人都会饮茶。根据那些参与铺设美国横贯东西大铁路的华人劳工的后代诉说，他们曾祖父们的劳工和约里条规列明了他们每天在铁道上工作时会有热茶供应。华人厨师定时把热茶送到铁道上。西方人劳工们喝了没有煮过的河水，常受疾病困扰，而华人劳工们能避免患病，相信都是热茶的功劳。

Tea-making set

活水还须活火烹，
自临钓石汲深情。
大瓢贮月归春瓮，
小勺分江入夜瓶。

宋朝诗人苏东坡

Living water must be boiled
  with living fire.
Fetching deep clear water
  from the Fishing Rock.
My bucket saved the moon
  into a jar for spring,
And my small scoop divided
  the stream into a bottle
    for the evening.

Su Dongpo, poet, Sung Dynasty

药

从食物营养学的角度来看，华人并没有仔细区分食物药物。对身体有益的，是药物，同时也是食物。公元6世纪的医药学家孙思邈曾说：'凡欲治疗，先以食疗；既食疗不愈，后乃用药耳'。

林语堂、*The Importance of Living*

世界各国的唐人街至今仍可找到中药铺。早年的海外华人，尤其是女性，喜欢到中药铺买上一包包药材，回家炖汤给家人，以此强身健体、促进血液循环、化痰祛瘀。母亲会把家中每天常喝的补汤方子教给女儿或儿媳；这成了海外华人传承的传统文化的一部分。

Herbal shop, Singapore, mid-1900s

Food and drinks stall, Indochina, late 1800s/early 1900s

herbs

Taking then the broader view of food as nourishment, the Chinese do not
draw any distinction between food and medicine. What is good for the
body is medicine and at the same time food... An early medical writer, Sun
Semiao (sixth century AD) says, 'A true doctor first finds out the cause of
the disease, and having found that out, he tries to cure it first by food.
When food fails, then he prescribes medicine.'

Lin Yutang, *The Importance of Living*

Every Chinatown in the world still has at least one herbal
shop that sells traditional herbs and medicine. The early
generations of overseas Chinese, especially women, would
visit the Chinese herbalist to buy packets of herbs to make
tonic soups to strengthen one's constitution, improve blood
circulation or rid the lungs of phlegm. Mothers used to pass
to their daughters and daughters-in-law recipes for tonic
soups that were drunk as part of the daily meal. Such soups
are part of the heritage of every Chinese overseas.

Reception dinner, Vancouver, British Columbia, Canada, c. 1910

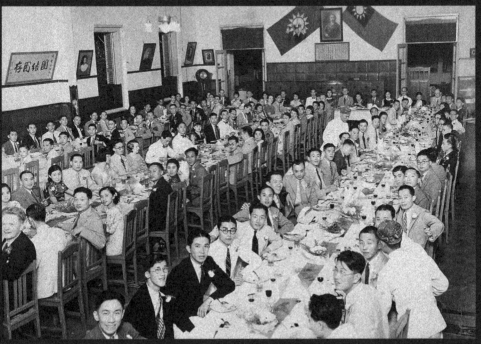

Student dinner, Jakarta, Indonesia, c. 1937

the joy of eating

Peace, prosperity and harmony or happiness is the theme of a Chinese New Year reunion dinner. This is the most important family meal, for which Chinese often travel countless distances so that they can join their families on New Year's Eve.

Australia, mid-1900s

The overseas Chinese from southern China attached great significance to certain food eaten during the New Year. Cantonese sojourners were born poets who loved the sound of words and the musicality of rhymes; besides writing poems expressing their longing for home and their loneliness in Gold Mountain, they also composed rhymes that celebrated the food eaten during the New Year. Mandarin oranges are a must for Chinese New Year because the Cantonese word for orange is *kum* (gold). Red dates are auspicious as well. A steamed whole chicken offered to the gods or ancestors during prayers always has a red date in its upturned beak, and a rhyme goes:

Eating red dates makes every year a good year.

Another important New Year dish is black mushrooms stewed with dried oysters (*ho si*, good deeds) and black moss (*fatt choy*, prosperity).

Mushrooms, oysters and black moss;
Prosper hugely, prosper easily.

Prawns are called *ha* in Cantonese, a word synonymous with laughter and joyous celebration.

Eat prawns, eat prawns,
For laughter big and small.

Early generations of overseas Chinese ate porridge with a dish of raw fish marinated with wine or lime juice. Later, eating fish became obligatory during New Year for fish symbolises prosperity.

Have prosperity, have prosperity.

Family dinner, Singapore, mid-1900s

享食之乐

平安富贵、合家欢乐是华人农历新年团圆饭的主题。这是每年最重要的一次家庭聚餐；华人为了在除夕夜与家人团聚，无论身处多么遥远的地方，都会赶回家过年。

来自中国南部的海外华人给新年吃的一些食物赋予了好兆头。广东侨民是天生的诗人，喜欢广东话那种像音乐韵调的语调；他们除了写诗表达思乡之情和在旧金山的孤独，也会写关于新年食物的诗。橘子是过年少不了的东西；广东话念kum（金）。红枣也是吉祥物品。祭拜祖先或是神灵时所献上的鸡，喉里总要含上一粒红枣。母亲和祖母们吃团圆饭时总会念：

吃红枣，年年好。

另外两项重要的过年食品是黑蘑菇炖干蚝（'好事'）和发菜（'发财'）。

虾在广东话里叫ha，暗示着笑声和欢庆。

吃虾吃虾，嘻哈大笑。

最早几代的海外华人吃粥时总是要配上一碟淋上中国酒或酸柑的生鱼。后来，因为'鱼'有富贵有余的意思，过年时吃鱼成了必事。

有鱼，有余。

The Lotus Restaurant, Paris, France, early 1900s

印度:近邻

华人移居印度的历史可以追溯到18世纪。1770年代，第一个定居印度的华人杨大钊到了加尔各答。这些早期华人移民大概都是海员和契约劳工。

到了19世纪，加尔各答的华人人数增加到了805人。1900年代初，这人数增加到了九千人，而到了1962年的中印冲突时期，居住在加尔各答的华人大约有14,000名。印度国会1962年通过法令，由于中国与印度交战，不承认中国移民的后代的公民权。在这艰难时期，几千人被遣送回国，其他人则前往欧洲、北美洲和澳洲。在拉贾斯坦邦的约两千名印度华人遭到拘禁。到了1970年代，印度华人人数减少到了11,000千人。

20世纪早期来到印度的华人大多定居在印度西部。加尔各答是他们在印度东部的主要据居地。少数华人也聚居在新德里、孟买和班加罗尔等地。印度华人大多是广东人、客家人和湖北人。

India: A Close Neighbour

The history of the Chinese in India can be traced back to the
when the first Chinese Atchew or Achii (or Yang Dazhao)
arrived in Calcutta in the 1770s. These early Chinese
migrants were likely sailors or indentured labourers.

By the nineteenth century, the Chinese population in
Calcutta had grown to 805. In the early 1900s, this number
was 9,000, and by 1962, during the Sino-Indian conflict,
there were 14,000 Chinese in Calcutta. An act of the Indian
Parliament in 1962 denied citizenship to descendants of
settlers from a country at war with India, and during this
difficult period, several thousands were deported while
others left for Europe, North America and Australia. Two
thousand Indian Chinese were interned in the state of
Rajasthan and by the 1970s, the Chinese population in
India had fallen to 11,000.

The Chinese who came in the early part of twentieth century
settled mostly in the western part of India. In the east,
Calcutta is the main centre of their presence. Cities with
smaller Chinese populations include New Delhi, Mumbai
and Bangalore, where they are mainly the Cantonese, the
Hakkas and the Hubeinese.

加拿大：融入主流

战后时期的加拿大，有钱华人纷纷搬离唐人街，搬入更好的新居。华人如其他加拿大人一样，也想拥有自己的房子。但是，他们的选择其实并不多。一位**Gee**先生看中了一栋位于克茨兰奴的房子，下了定金；但周围白人邻居听到有华人要搬入这所房子的消息，联名上书政府反对。**Gee**先生最后只好选择离开，所下的定金也没能拿回来。

钟德妮《小姨太的子女》

我从没意识到这（种族歧视）问题，直到我读了历史，才知道原来我祖父母的那个时代，他们无法融入白人主流社会。他们被排斥于其外，不能成为正式公民，不能拥有自己的房产，没有投票权。现在我回想起来，这些都是他们那时代的一部分，如今，仅仅几十年之后，我在总理手下工作。

钟德妮

钟德妮的祖父母生活在加拿大种族歧视现象严重的时期。不过到了1960年代之后，加拿大开始推行多元种族政策。钟德妮自幼在卑诗省长大，担任了加拿大总理皮艾尔·杜鲁多的经济策略顾问。

自加拿大太平洋铁路公司1800年代雇佣上千个华人移民劳工以来，加拿大华人已走过一段长旅。他们在政治、艺术和文化各个领域都扮演举足轻重的角色，已成为加拿大社会不可分割的一部分。在加拿大出生的第二代华裔李亮汉担任了哥伦比亚大学的校长，而华裔林思齐当上了卑诗省的副总督。在各城市里，如温哥华和多伦多，唐人街被视为珍贵的民族文化遗产。随着家人于1942年移民到加拿大的华人伍冰枝，于2000年就职成为加拿大总督。

Canada:
The Road to Acceptance

The postwar trend in Chinatown was for anyone who could afford better accommodation to move out. Like other Canadian families, Chinese families had aspirations to own their own homes. However, they did not necessarily have their choice of neighbourhoods. Mr Gee had put down a deposit on a house in Kitsilano. When white neighbours got wind that a Chinese family wanted to move in, they amassed a petition against him. He walked away, losing his deposit.

Denise Chong, *The Concubine's Children*

I didn't realise the extent of it [racism], until I did my history, that my grandparents lived in Canada at a time when they could not participate in White society. They were excluded from it: they could not take out citizenship, they couldn't own land, they couldn't vote. And when I think back, that's part of their legacy... And, within a few decades, here I was, working for the prime minister.

Denise Chong

Denise Chong's grandparents lived through a period in Canadian history when the Chinese were disenfranchised. However, from the late 1960s onwards, the Canadian government adopted a policy of multiculturalism. Chong, who grew up in British Columbia, went on to become an economic advisor to prime minister Pierre Trudeau.

Chinese Canadians have travelled a long road since the days of the Canadian Pacific Railroad Company, which employed thousands of migrant labourers during the late 1800s. Chinese Canadians are an intrinsic part of the fabric of Canadian society and play prominent roles in government, the arts and culture. Second-generation citizen Robert Lee was the chancellor of the University of British Columbia, and David Lam See-chai was Lieutenant-Governor of British Columbia. Chinatowns in cities like Vancouver and Toronto are treasured neighbourhoods. In 2000, Madame Adrienne Clarkson, who arrived in Canada with her family in 1942, was appointed the Governor General.

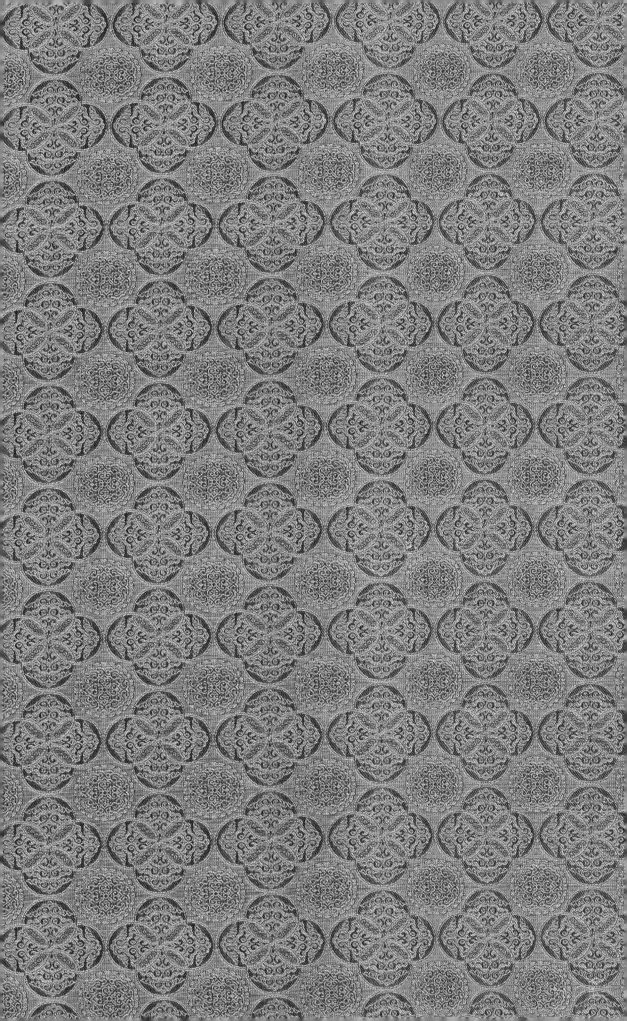

Rituals

Since the earliest days, we have continued to worship the gods and practise in one form or another the rituals our grandparents brought from their home villages, adapting these ceremonies to fit the circumstances of our adopted countries. In America, we pray in private whereas in Southeast Asia, our rituals are visible in the temples and the public conduct of our births, marriages and funerals.

最早时期，我们延续了中国拜神的习俗，以各种方式继续着祖辈从家乡传过来的仪式。我们为了符合异国的需要，把这些仪式稍稍作了改变。在美国，我们在家里私下祭拜；而在东南亚，我们仍在寺庙里举行祭典，公开举行庆生、婚礼、葬礼。

Extended family portrait, Vancouver, British Columbia, Canada, c. 1910

妹妹满月时，大人给她穿上一件粉红色衣服。衣服之所以是粉红色，是因为
粉红色最接近象征吉祥的红色。她还穿戴了几个小小的金首饰，象征着好运
长寿。一只称为'金猪'的大烧猪，摆放在客厅里的架子上；它前方摆着蜡
烛和其他祭拜物品。父亲开始祭拜及祈求神灵大发慈悲，保佑这出生不久的
婴儿。接着纸钱烧了，金猪也切成小块分给亲戚朋友；其他分给大家的食品
还包括了姜丝、馒头和红鸡蛋。这些都象征着好运、健康和幸福。

1930年出生于夏威夷的华人

When Sister was a month old,
she was dressed in a pink dress.
The dress was pink because it was
nearest to red, the lucky colour of
the Chinese. She also wore some gold
trinkets symbolising good luck and
long life. On that day we had a large
roasted pig, called a 'golden pig'. It
was put on a stand in the parlour and
in front of it were placed candles and
other ceremonial articles. Father then
bowed and prayed that the gods be
generous and that they protect the
new-born babe. After that the paper
money was burned. Then the pig was
cut into slices to distribute to friends
and relatives. Preserved ginger, buns
and red-coloured eggs were also
distributed. These were all symbols
of good luck, health and happiness.

A Hawaiian-born Chinese, 1930

Quong Tart and
Margaret Tart,
Australia, late 1800s

Husband and wife, America, c. 1884

marriage

In the early 1900s, when many Chinese marriages were still arranged, parents would consult an astrologer or temple priest to check if the couple's horoscopes clashed. If their horoscopes matched, the astrologer would find an auspicious date for their wedding.

Miss Ong Geok Neo... knelt before the altar to offer the gods and ancestors libations of tea and wine. Then she kowtowed three times, knocking her head upon the wooden floor, and the ritual of combing the maiden's hair began... Her elder aunt snipped off the ends of her long black locks, combing as she sang in provincial Cantonese:

> Loy-ah-loy! Nae first comb, comb each hair
>> Till husband and wife grow white and old.
> Nae second comb, comb it long
>> Till sons, grandsons and great grandsons
> Fill and bless your days.
>> Nae comb, comb it thrice!
> May health and wealth and honour
>> Come your lord and master's way.

Suchen Christine Lim, *Fistful of Colours*

Cut off from women from their homeland, many Chinese men married non-Chinese women and established families with children of mixed parentage. Many men and women whose names went unrecorded in history defied tradition and prejudice to marry outside their ethnic communities. The marriage of the eminent Australian-Chinese Quong Tart to Margaret Scarlett in 1886 was extensively reported by the press, and a poem composed in their honour.

> ...May peace and love surround thy life,
>> And never from thy home depart
> May God keep far from thee all strife,
>> Preserve and bless thy loving wife,
>> And thee, Quong Tart.

Margaret Tart, *The Life of Quong Tart*

Bridal carriage, Ternate, Moluccan Islands, c. 1890

Trevor and Mary Jack, Australia, c. 1943

Quong Tart and his family, Australia, c. 1892

The children of mixed marriages were usually brought up as Chinese, and one or more sons were sent back to their home village in China for their education.

My father said he went back to China when he was eight years old with his father (and) returned when he was nineteen years old. He said he has two mothers… He stayed with this Chinese woman (who) is very nice to him… 'China mother very, very good'. He said she treated him just like her own son. He said, 'Hawaiian mother good too, treat me good, but China mother very, very good'. He is more used to her ways… You see he likes Chinese ways and he was brought up in a Chinese manner.

The daughter of a Chinese-Hawaiian who had been taken to China as a boy, 1931

The establishment of families in new lands turned the sojourners into settlers, and their homes changed from rooms shared with male companions to family units in shophouses and apartments, or houses in the suburbs and countryside. Wealthy men built grand mansions. Later, when immigration laws were relaxed, more Chinese men were able to bring their wives to their new country. After the 1906 earthquake in San Francisco destroyed all immigration records, the Chinese in San Francisco were able to bring over their families from China.

The children who grew up and went to schools in America, Canada and Australia became second-generation Chinese. They moved away from the work of their parents to make their mark in professional, scientific and artistic fields.

婚嫁

1900年代初，许多夫妻还经由媒妁之言促成；双方父母请算命先生或庙里的师父算一下双方的生辰八字是否相冲。若生辰八字吻合，算命先生就会选个黄道吉日举行婚礼。

> 黄玉娘在神台前跪下，为神灵和祖先斟茶敬酒。叩了三次响头之后，梳头仪式正式开始...她的大姨把她黑色长发的末梢剪掉，边剪边以广东腔唱道：
> 一梳梳到尾，
> 二梳白发齐眉，
> 三梳儿孙满堂，
> 四梳梳到四条银
> 笋尽标齐。

林苏贞，Fistful of Colours

华人男子与家乡女子异地而处，缺乏联系。他们许多于是娶了不同种族的女子，生下混血儿。许多连名字都没有被记载下来的男男女女，抵受传统习俗的压力和种族之间的歧视，与不同种族的人结了婚。梅光达（**Quong Tart**）和**Margaret Scarlett**的婚姻曾在澳洲引起了平面媒体的广泛报道，还有人为了纪念这婚礼，写了一首诗。

> ...愿宁静而恩爱充满着他们的生活
> 永远不从他们的家中离开
> 愿上帝保佑他们远离争吵
> 永远祝福你美丽的妻子
> 和你－梅光达。

Margaret Tart, The Life of Quong Tart

通婚所生下的孩子通常会以华人身份给带大，而且至少会有一个儿子被送回中国老家受教育。

> 我父亲说，他八岁时跟着他的父亲回到中国，十九岁才回来。他说他有两个母亲...他跟一位对他很好的华人女性一起住...'中国母亲非常非常好'...他说她像对亲生儿子那样对待他。他说：'夏威夷母亲也很好，待我很好，但中国母亲非常非常好。' 他比较习惯她的方式...他喜欢中国习俗，他是以中国传统方式带大的。

一位在1931年童年时被带回中国的夏威夷华人的女儿这样说

许多旅居海外的华人在新的国度里成家立业，也从此定居当地；他们本来和其他男性伙伴合租地方住，定居后搬进了郊区或乡村里的商品房和楼房。有钱人还为自己造了豪宅。后来，随着移民政策的放宽，更多华人男子可携带妻子入境。1906年，旧金山的一场地震毁掉了当地所有的移民档案，旧金山的华人因此得以将自己的家人也从中国接过去。

那些在美国、加拿大和澳洲等地长大、求学的子女成了海外华人的第二代。他们走出了海外华人的传统行业，在各个专业、科学和艺术领域创造自己的历史。

Chinese family in local costumes, Java, Indonesia, c. 1867

American family portrait, c. 1914

Canadian family portrait, c. 1925

Mausoleum of the 72 Martyrs, Guangzhou

Ching Ming, Washington, DC

Funeral, Singapore, c. 1900

honouring those before us

All sojourners longed to return home in their old age and to die in their villages. Should they die in the foreign land, they wanted to be buried in their homeland. Returning the dead to their home village was one of the functions of clan associations. The Changhou Tang in nineteenth century San Francisco, for example, sent the coffins and bones of gold miners back to their villages for burial.

Pick up my bones and take them home.

A badly injured railroad builder to his friends

Accidents, avalanches and the bitter cold in the Sierra Nevada killed hundreds of Chinese railroad builders as they worked on the American transcontinental railroad. Years after its completion, some of these workers made the arduous journey through the mountains to search for the remains of their friends. These expeditions were called *jup seen you* (retrieving deceased friends) or *jup kuak* (retrieving bones). Digging beneath heaps of stones near the tracks that were marked by a wooden stake, they would find a skeleton and a wax-sealed bottle with a strip of cloth inside. The Chinese characters written on the cloth stated the dead man's name, birth date and home district. Such expeditions shipped back to China more than 1,000 railroad workers who had died along the tracks.

Funeral, Padang, Sumatra, c. 1900

Family altar, Singapore, c. 1960

Ching Ming is when we honour our ancestors. Between
the first and fifteenth of the third month of the lunar
calendar, families pray for the departed at home and
at the cemetery. Graves are swept and cleaned by the
cemetery's caretakers, and the grass on the grave
mounds is cut. Families offer food and wine or tea, and
burn gold and silver paper.

The soul of the deceased is believed to enjoy the meal during the
worship, which usually lasts for an hour, and at the end, a 'pak puay'
is asked for. Permission to end the worship must be sought from the
soul by tossing two coins in the air, and these must show a head and
a tail as they land on the floor. Two tails show that it is amused, but it
is not ready to stop eating. Two heads signified that it is annoyed at
being hurried...

I remember such a worship at which I was asked by my grandmother
to perform the *pak puay*, recalling too how impatient I was to end
it. I was anxious to end it because we could all only eat after the
sembahyang (prayers). I was hungry for lunch, and at the third throw
as I picked the coins up I felt like turning over one of the heads into
a tail. But the rather icy look in my grandfather's eyes in the large
photograph which hung conspicuously over the altar made me hand
the coins to my grandmother! However, I succeeded in tossing a head
and a tail at the next throw.

Felix Chia, *The Babas*

Family altar, Guangdong

祭祖

所有旅居海外的华人都希望年迈时能回故乡，死于出生之地。就算客死异乡，他们也希望自己最后被埋葬在故乡土地。同乡会馆的功能之一就是把身死他乡的人的尸骨送回故乡。比如说19世纪建于旧金山的长后堂，就负责将华人金矿工的棺材及骨骸送回家乡安葬。

> 拾起我的尸骨，把它带回家。

一个身受重伤的铁道建筑华工这样嘱咐自己的朋友

上百个华人劳工在内华达山里修建横贯美国大陆的大铁路时，死于意外、雪崩或严寒。铁路工程完工数年后，一些活下来的劳工又重新踏上了穿越内华达山的艰辛旅程，寻找他们死去多年的朋友的骸骨。这些旅程被称为'拾先友'或'拾骨'。他们在铁路附近、有木桩做标记的石碓挖掘，发现埋着的尸骨和装着布条的瓶子。瓶子里的布条上记录了死者的名字、生辰、故乡。他们最后找到了超过一千个死在铁路旁的工人的尸骸送回了中国。

Ancestral tablet, Guangzhou

到了清明节，我们会到祖先的坟上扫墓、祭拜。从农历三月初一到十五的这段期间，家家户户都会在家里或坟场为已故亲人祈福。坟场的看护人会打理坟墓，为坟墓除草。家人会到坟上献上食物、酒茶，烧金银纸。

> 葬礼的祭拜仪式通常长达一小时，一般传统认为死者的魂体会在这段期间享受供桌上的祭品；祭拜仪式到了尾声，须讨 **pak puay**：祭拜是否可以结束须征求死者的同意－抛两枚硬币，如果朝上的是一正一背才表示死者同意结束祭祀。两枚硬币都背面朝上表示他开心，但还没吃饱；两枚都正面朝上表示他不高兴被催促。我还记得一次这样的祭拜仪式，我被祖母叫来讨 **pak puay**。当时我很不耐烦，想尽快完成仪式。我之所以心急是因为我们要到仪式结束才可以吃饭。我肚子饿极了，抛到第三次的时候，我好想把两枚正面朝上的硬币的其中一个换成背面朝上。但祖父在挂在祭台上的大照片里的表情非常严肃，我最后还是将硬币原封不动地交给了祖母。终于在下一次抛的时候，成功地抛到了一正一背。

Felix Chia, The Babas

Jin De Yuen Temple, Jakarta, c. 1880

欧洲:远方家园

自19世纪末，华人通过陆路或海路抵达欧洲。英法联军第一次世界大战时雇佣了大约十四万名华籍劳工在西线从事非战斗性工作。

一位负责管理华人劳工的英国军官在战斗中吸到毒气，动弹不得。尽管被德军包围，华人劳工守护着他，与德军作战。这名英国军官最后获救了，但活下来的华人劳工只有几个。这名军官说：'我这条命是华人劳工救回来的'。

二战后，特别是1980年代，从中国和东南亚过来的华人移民浪潮一波接一波。如今华人的身影遍布丹麦、荷兰、比利时和意大利等20多个国家。

俄国

从1860年代起到第一次世界大战，成千上万的华人劳工涌入俄国，从事铁路、木材和矿场等工业。有名的"义成"公司招募了超过两万名华人到斯摩棱斯克伐木；华人苦力也在黑龙江北挖金矿，在海参崴帮助建设海港。华人劳工都超时工作，还得听任突如其来的使唤。在Kizal的煤矿场，老板组建了一支华人监察队，专门负责殴打虐待工人，而凡是罢工活动都会被强力镇压。

1917年俄国王室被革命推翻之后，在接下来的动荡中，约九万名在俄国欧洲地区的华人失去了工作，在西伯利亚的三万名左右的华人也失了业。他们许多人沿着西伯利亚大铁路一路乞讨回乡，也有几千人加入了红军。

俄国共产党政府上台执政后，华人学生开始陆续来到莫斯科，之中包括了邓小平和后来的台湾政府总统蒋经国。1950年代，在俄国的华人人数达到了350,00名；1960年代中俄两国关系冷淡下来，这个人数下降了。随着1980年代末俄国的开放，华人又开始进入俄国。

Europe: Distant Homes

Since the late nineteenth century, the Chinese had arrived
in Europe from overland or by sea. During World War I, the
British and French governments recruited 140,000 Chinese
labourers for non-combat work on the Western Front.

During one battle, a British officer commanding a group of Chinese
labourers was gassed and could not move. Though surrounded by German
soldiers, the Chinese stood round him and fought the Germans. The officer
was eventually saved by relief forces, but all except a few of the Chinese
were killed. 'I owe my life', he said, 'to the labourers under my command'.

Tuk Min-Chien TZ, *China Awakened*

After World War II, particularly in the 1980s, waves of
new immigrants arrived from China and Southeast Asia.
Today, they live in more than 20 European states including
Denmark, the Netherlands, Belgium and Italy.

Russia

From the 1860s to the First World War, thousands of
Chinese labourers arrived in Russia to work in the railroad,
timber and coalmining industries. One company, Yicheng,
sent over 20,000 men to fell trees in Smolensk, and coolies
mined gold north of the Heilongjiang River and built the
harbour at Vladivostock. Chinese workers were overworked
and subjected to arbitrary actions. In the Kizal coalmines,
the company bosses created a Chinese police force that beat
and tortured workers, and strikes were brutally suppressed.

In the unrest following the fall of the Russian monarchy in
1917, 90,000 Chinese workers were made jobless in Russia's
European provinces, and 30,000 in Siberia. Many begged
their way home along the trans-Siberian Railway, while
thousands joined the Red Army.

When the Communist government took over, Chinese
students started to arrive in Moscow, among them Deng
Xiaoping and Chiang Ching-kuo (later the president of
Taiwan). In the 1950s, the Chinese community in Russia
numbered nearly 350,000, but when relations between the
two countries turned cold in the 1960s, these numbers
declined. With the opening up of Russia at the end of the
1980s, the Chinese returned in great numbers again.

英国

我们许多人都应该曾听过父母那些喋喋不休、让我们不胜其烦的念叨：做事做得和别人一样好还不够，我们必须比其他人做得还要好。我们可以很自豪的说，大致上，我们的确做到了这一点。

英籍华商格雷厄姆·陈

孙逸仙医生（孙中山）**1896**年到伦敦为中国革命活动筹款时，那里居住着大约**400**名中国移民。到了**1911**年，在英格兰和威尔士居住的华人居民都各有**1,300**名左右。不过，当地隐藏着的反华情绪被街头小报所诱导，爆发了一些反华活动，在卡地夫一地的所有**33**间华人洗衣铺毁于一旦。

二战后，从中国及英联邦属地前来的华籍工人和学生扩大了英国的华人社群。近几年，中国大陆来的移民不断进入英国；他们许多是偷渡客。**2002**年，第一个由华人领导的反种族歧视观察组织－'民权'，在伦敦成立了。

法国

第一次世界大战时，英国和法国政府为了弥补劳工短缺的情况，从中国招募劳工。最终估计有约十四万'华工团'的队伍到了法国。战后，大部分华人劳工被遣送回国，但其中有三千人留在了法国，从事航空和冶金业的工作。这首批华人移民之后，在**1919**年至**1920**年间，大约有**1,600**百名华人学生来到法国勤工俭学。他们包括了邓小平、周恩来、陈毅、向警予（中共第一任妇女部部长）等人，后来都成为了中国共产党内的重要领导人。

1930年代，另一批从浙江来的华人移民到达了法国的那普勒斯和马赛。许多华人在二战之后的艰难时期带着他们的法国妻子和子女回了中国，其他一些人则去了荷兰、比利时和意大利。如今在法国的华人社群相当兴旺，包括了许多法国的专业人士、艺术家和作家。其中最出名的一个当属诺贝尔文学奖得主高行健。

Britain

Many of us will have been exasperated by the constant refrain from our parents that it is not enough for us to be as good as anyone else, we must be better than anyone else. We can be proud that we have, by and large, proved to be exactly that.

Graham Chan, a British-born Chinese

There were about 400 Chinese immigrants when Dr Sun Yat-sen arrived in London in 1896 to raise funds for his revolutionary cause. By 1911, the number of Chinese settlers was about 1,300 in England and Wales. However, anti-Asian demonstrations stoked by the tabloid press led to the destruction of all 33 Chinese laundries in Cardiff.

In the post-war years, Chinese workers and students from China and the British Commonwealth increased the size of the Chinese community. Recent years have seen an influx of arrivals from China, many of whom are illegal immigrants. In 2002, the first Chinese-led anti-racism monitoring group, Min Quan ('Civil Rights'), was launched in London.

France

The labour shortage during World War I prompted the British and French governments to recruit Chinese workers. Eventually, an estimated 140,000 workers of the Chinese Labour Corps came to France. After the war, these labourers were repatriated except for 3,000 who remained, working in the aeronautics and metallurgical industries. This first group of immigrants was soon followed by one of students—between 1919 and 1920, about 1,600 students arrived in France. Students like Deng Xiaoping, Zhou Enlai, Chen Yi and Xiang Jingyu (the first director of the Women's Bureau) later became key leaders in the Chinese Communist Party.

In the 1930s, a third group of immigrants from Zhejiang province arrived at the ports of Naples and Marseilles. In the difficult post-World War II period, many Chinese took their French wives and children back to China while others went to the Netherlands, Belgium and Italy. Today there is a thriving community of Chinese artists and writers in France, the most famous of whom is Gao Xingjian, the Nobel Prize winner for Literature.

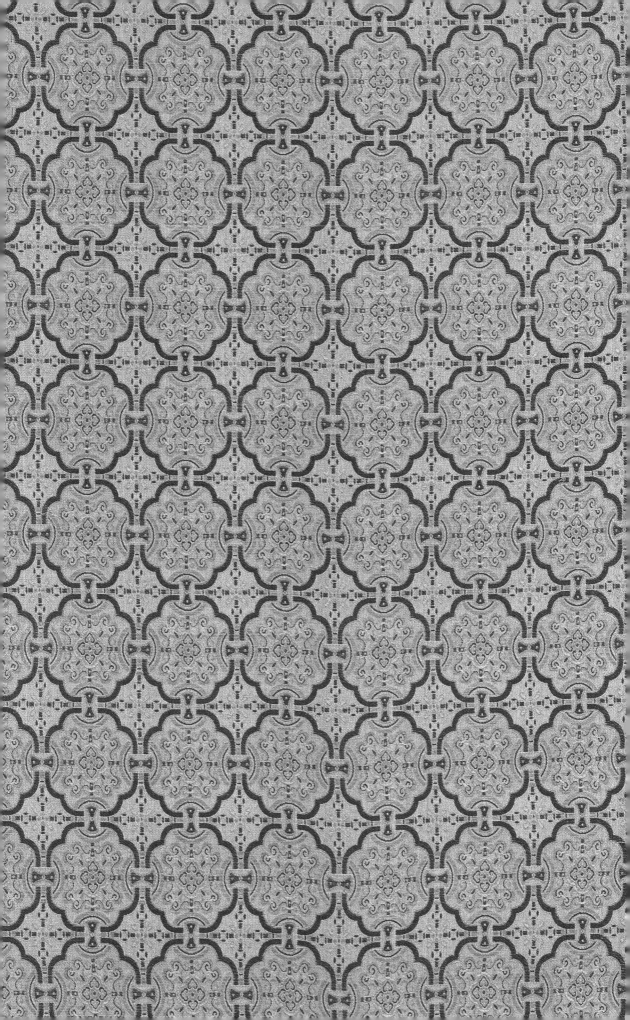

Trailblazers

When our forebears left China to hew out a
new future and fortune, they blazed across the
world and opened paths for themselves and their
descendants. The fruits of their labour became the
inheritance of those who came after them.

我们的先辈们离开中国，到海外寻找新的未
来和财富时，踏遍了全世界，为自己和子孙
们开辟了全新的途径。他们辛劳的成果，化
成了他们后代所继承的宝贵遗产。

前人种苗，后人收果。

广东谚语

LIM NEE SOON RUBBER FACTORY

洪水港养顺庄通益树琠房

Rubber and pineapple baron Lim Nee Soon at his plantation, Singapore, c. 1916

The generation in front
sows the seeds;
The generation behind
harvests the fruit.

Cantonese proverb

Singapore, early 1900s

tan kah kee

Tan Kah Kee (1874–1961), the Rubber King or Henry Ford of Malaya, rose from the collapse of his father's rice business and went on to build a business empire that employed 32,000 people. An entrepreneur who ventured into uncharted waters, he owned ships at a time when non-British subjects in colonial Singapore were not allowed to do so by becoming a naturalised British subject. His ships ensured a steady supply of rice for his mills, and his pineapple and rubber products were shipped directly to markets in the West. By doing so, he broke the European rubber trading monopoly in Singapore.

Tan donated millions to projects such as the China Relief Fund and founded many schools, including the Chinese High School in Singapore and Xiamen University. He also crossed political boundaries fearlessly—in 1910, he cut off his queue to show his opposition to the Manchu regime. In 1916, he changed his citizenship and became a British subject. In 1950, he crossed a third boundary and renounced his British citizenship when he left Singapore to return to China. When he died in Beijing, the Chinese government accorded him a state funeral as Chinese communities around the world held memorial services.

陈嘉庚

陈嘉庚(1874-1961年)是橡胶大王，誉为'马来亚亨利·福特'。他在父亲的米店生意破产后，自己重新建立了巨大商业王国。他是勇于开拓新领域的企业家。当时新加坡还是英国殖民地，非英国子民不得拥有船只；他于是成了英国国籍，从而得以拥有船队。这支船队确保他所经营的磨坊有稳定的稻米供应，他公司生产的黄梨和橡胶产品也得以被直接运送到西方市场。陈嘉庚通过这些生意手法打破了当时欧洲人垄断新加坡橡胶贸易的局面。

陈嘉庚曾捐出上百万元给众多公益组织，包括中国赈灾基金会；他也创办了许多学校，如新加坡的华侨中学、中国的厦门大学等。他也无畏地越过政治界限：他1910年剪掉了辫子，公开表明反对满清政府的立场。1916年，他换了国籍，成了英国公民。1950年，他离开新加坡回到中国时，放弃了英国国籍，从而越过了第三个界限。他1961年逝世于北京时，中国政府为他举行了国葬，世界各地的华人都为他举行了追悼会。

Florida, late 1800s/early 1900s

lue gim gong

Lue Gim Gong (1859–1925) literally sowed the seeds of the
fortunes of American farmers in Florida's fruit industry.
In the nineteenth century, citrus farms were plagued by
insects, disease and frost. Lue, who arrived in America
in 1868 at the age of 10, was the first horticulturalist
to cultivate a frost-resistant variety of orange. The Lue
Gim Gong Orange won the Wilder Medal because it could
withstand frost and be shipped over long distances without
spoiling. Lue also developed a frost-resistant grapefruit.

Lue devoted his life to horticulture. When he returned to
China after his long sojourn in America, he refused to marry
the bride his parents had chosen for him. He came back to
America, remained single and died an American, and his
name lives on in Florida's fruit industry.

吕金功

吕金功(1859-1925年)可说是真的为佛罗里达州的美国水果种植人
播下了财富的种子。19世纪时的柑橘种植园被各种害虫、水果疾病
和霜害肆虐。1868年，十岁的吕金功来到了美国，之后成了第一个
成功培植出抗霜柑橘的人。'吕金功柑橘'能耐抗霜冻，即使经过
长途运送也不会腐烂，因而获得了'耘荒者'奖章。吕金功也培植
出了一种抗霜的柚子。

吕金功把一生奉献给了水果种植业。他在美国居住多年后，回到中
国；但他拒绝迎娶父母为他选定的结婚对象。他又回到了美国，继
续过着单身生活，以美国人身份在美国去世，而他的名字一直流传
于佛罗里达州水果种植业。

Hartford, Connecticut, late 1800s/early 1900s

yung wing

Many overseas Chinese returned to China to help the country modernise. Yung Wing (1828–1912) was one of the forerunners in western learning. Aided by missionaries, Yung left China at 12 to study in America. Coming from a poor background, he resolved to acquire the knowledge needed by his homeland.

I wanted the utmost freedom of action to avail myself of every opportunity to do the greatest good in China... To be sure, I was poor, but I would not allow my poverty to gain the upper hand and compel me to barter away my inward convictions of duty...

In 1854, Yung became the first Chinese graduate of Yale University. Returning to China, he worked as a translator for the Shanghai customs service, became a prosperous tea merchant and convinced the Qing government to send students to America for further studies. In 1872, Yung became the deputy commissioner of the Chinese Educational Mission, which sent 120 students to Hartford, Connecticut. His mission bore fruit.

Yung also helped Shanghai with its plans to mechanise its textile industry. He later married an American and became an American citizen.

容闳

许多海外华人回中国协助国家迈向现代化。容闳（1828–1912年）便是倡导'西学'的先驱之一。他十二岁时得到教会的资助，离开中国到美国留学。他家境贫困，下定了决心学好祖国所须的知识。

我要最大限度的行动自由，利用每个为中国带来巨大好处的机会…当然，我很穷；但我不会让贫穷占上风，迫使我放弃自己内心的信仰。

1854年，容闳成了耶鲁大学历史上第一个华人毕业生。回到中国之后，他当了上海海关翻译员，当了成功的茶商，说服清政府派遣学生到美国留学。容闳1872年被清政府任命为'幼童出洋肄业局'副监督。这肄业局派了120名幼童前往美国康涅狄格州的首府哈福特市。这项计划获得了丰硕的成果。

容闳还曾帮助上海第一间现代纺织厂购买所需器材。他后来娶了美国人，成了美国公民。

Aw Boon Haw and Aw Boon Par, early 1900s

the aw brothers

Aw Boon Haw (1882–1954) and his brother, Boon Par (1888–1944), were born in Myanmar. Their father owned a herbal shop and after his death, Boon Haw managed the business, while Boon Par apprenticed himself to a pharmacist. According to folklore, this man had given Boon Par a recipe for a pain-relieving ointment before he died. The Aw brothers used this to concoct Ban Kim Ewe (Ten Thousand Golden Oil).

Tiger Balm

After World War I, Boon Par created Red Tiger Balm, while Boon Haw was the marketing genius who sold Tiger Balm to herbal shops throughout Southeast Asia. Their business grew rapidly; in 1926, Boon Haw moved to Singapore and diversified into newspapers and banking. Boon Haw founded *Sin Chew Jit Poh*, the first of a group of newspapers in the region. This was followed by newspapers in Hong Kong, Taiwan and Thailand. After World War II, he founded Chung Khiaw Bank. The Aw brothers gave generously to charities. From 1929 to 1949, they donated over US$70 million to build schools and hospitals in China. In Singapore, they built the famed Haw Par Villa (Tiger Balm Gardens) in memory of their parents.

胡氏兄弟

胡文虎（1882-1954年）和弟弟胡文豹（1888-1944年）出生于缅甸。他们的父亲经营着一家药材铺，而在父亲过世后，文虎继承了药店，文豹则当了当地医师的学徒。根据民间传说，这位医师过世之前传给了文豹一个止痛药油的秘密配方，胡氏兄弟用这个配方制成了能治百病的药，称为'万金油'。

第一次世界大战后，文豹制成'虎标万金油'，而文虎则是把虎标万金油带入遍及全东南亚所有中药铺的商业奇才。生意扩展地很快；胡文虎1926年移居到新加坡，把业务扩充到办报和银行业。文虎首先在新加坡创立了《星洲日报》，是他之后在地区所办的一系列报纸的开始。二战后，他创立了崇侨银行。胡氏兄弟慷慨解囊，捐赠了大笔款项给各类慈善机构。从1929年到1949年，他们共捐献了超过七千万元美金，在中国建立学校医院。他们在新加坡斥资兴建了著名的'虎豹别墅'，以此纪念父母。

Political rally, Singapore, c. 1963

lee kuan yew

The founding prime minister of Singapore, Lee was born on 16 September 1923. He led Singapore's struggle for independence before becoming its prime minister in 1959.

Once in a long while, in the history of a people, there comes a moment of great change. Tonight is such a moment. Last Saturday saw the end of an era. This morning a new constitution was promulgated. We begin a new chapter in the history of Singapore.

Lee Kuan Yew on Singapore's new constitution, 3 June 1959

A descendant of the Hakkas of Dapu County, Lee initiated policies and directions that transformed the country from a colonial trading post into a thriving nation.

The past 24 years were not preordained. Nor is the future. There will be unexpected problems ahead, as there were in the past. They have to be met, grappled with, and resolved. For only a people willing to face up to their problems and are prepared to work with their leaders to meet unexpected hardships with courage and resolution deserve to thrive and to prosper.

Lee Kuan Yew on his sixtieth birthday

李光耀

新加坡的建国总理李光耀生于1923年9月16日。他领导了新加坡的独立运动，1959年成为总理。

在一国人民的历史之中，每过上一段时间，就会出现一次大转变的时刻。今晚就是这样的时刻。上星期六，我们亲眼见证了一个时代的结束。今天早上，我们颁布了一套新的宪法。我们正在翻开新加坡历史中新的一页。

李光耀1959年6月3日对新加坡的新宪法发表言论

李光耀是来自中国广东大埔县的客家人的后代。他的政策把新加坡从单纯的殖民贸易港口变成了经济繁荣的国家。

过去24年的成就并不是上天注定的。未来也不会是。以前有过预想不到的问题，以后也会有。对于这些困难，我们必须正视、进行搏斗、解决。因为只有愿意认真面对自身问题，做好心理准备同领袖一起合作，以勇气和决心面对预想不到的困难的人民，才有资格成功、富强。

李光耀六十岁寿辰讲话

chin sophonpanich

The son of a sawmill clerk, Chin Sophonpanich (1910–1988) founded Thailand's first finance company and later, the Bangkok Bank. He started out as a shop apprentice, working on a boat travelling between Bangkok and Ayudhya, then became a clerk in a construction company and later a lumber trader. When World War II ended, he established a finance company that offered foreign exchange services and remittance services, and co-founded the Bangkok Bank in 1944.

Having studied how the major European banks operated, Chin hired economists and professional bankers to run the bank. Forced into exile after a military coup, he returned to Thailand in 1964 and under his leadership, the bank played a significant role in Thailand's economic development.

陈弼臣

创办了泰国第一家金融公司和泰国盘谷银行的陈弼臣（1910-1988年）只是一个锯木厂书记员的儿子。他从一名在往来于曼谷和阿瑜陀城之间的轮船上打杂的普通店铺学徒做起，然后当了建筑公司的书记员，再后来成为了木材贸易商。二战结束后，他创建了一家金融公司，专门从事外汇兑换和汇款业务。1944年，他集资创办了盘谷银行。

陈弼臣研究了欧洲大型银行的运作方式，聘请了专业经济学家和银行家管理银行。他在一场军事政变后被迫离开泰国，1964年回到泰国。在他的领导之下，盘谷银行在泰国的经济发展中扮演了极其重要的角色。

oei tiong ham

Among the Chinese who became successful at plantation
agriculture in Southeast Asia, two stood out for having built
conglomerates based on sugarcane, rubber and pineapple—
Tan Kah Kee and Oei Tiong Ham (1866–1924). Oei was the
renowned Asian Sugar King of the Dutch East Indies. He
founded a multinational conglomerate that included sugar
plantations and refineries, a bank, warehouses and other
properties, and steamship companies. During the pre-
war period, the Oei Tiong Ham Concern was the first and
largest Chinese-owned business empire in Southeast Asia,
with offices in Bangkok, Calcutta, Singapore, Hong Kong,
Shanghai, London and New York.

黄仲涵

在东南亚从事种植业而获得成功的许多华人之中，最突出的当数陈
嘉庚和黄仲涵。他们两人都创建了以生产甘蔗、橡胶和黄梨为主的
大型商业组织。黄仲涵（1866-1924年）是荷属东印度群岛上著名
的'亚洲糖王'。他所创办的企业包括数家糖料种植园及炼糖厂、
一家银行、一间货仓及房地产发展公司，及数家货轮公司。战前，
建源贸易公司（黄仲涵的家族企业）已成为东南亚首个，也是最大
的由华人拥有的企业王国，在曼谷、加尔各达、新加坡、香港、上
海、伦敦和纽约都设有分行。

The Pyramide du Louvre, Paris, France

im pei

The architect IM Pei was born in 1917 and left China in 1934 as a 17-year-old to study architecture in the Massachusetts Imstitute of Technology, and later in Harvard. He became an American citizen in 1955, and in 1983, received the Pritzker Architecture Prize for his outstanding achievements.

...Pei has given this century some of its most beautiful interior spaces and exterior forms. Yet the significance of his work goes far beyond that. His concern has always been the surroundings in which his buildings rise... His versatility and skill in the use of materials approach the level of poetry.

The Pritzker Prize Jury

贝聿铭

建筑师贝聿铭在1934年十七岁时离开了中国，到麻省理工学院和哈福大学修读建筑设计学科。他于1955年成为美国公民，1983年因为杰出建筑设计成就获颁极具声望的'普利兹克'建筑设计奖。

这世纪最美丽的室内设计和室外建筑作品中，有好几项来自贝聿铭。但他作品所代表的意义远远超过这些设计本身。他最为关心的一直是他的建筑所处的周围环境...他在选择材料上的灵活性与技巧接近了创诗一般的境界。

普利兹克建筑设计奖评判团

adrienne clarkson

Born in Hong Kong in 1939, Madame Clarkson's family went to Canada in 1942. She grew up in Ottawa and obtained an MA in English Literature from the University of Toronto and did post-graduate work at the Sorbonne. Starting out as a journalist, Madame Clarkson has had a distinguished career in the arts and public service. She was appointed an Agent General for Ontario in Paris in the 1980s, and was an Officer of the Order of Canada in 1992. In 1999, she was sworn in as the Governor General of Canada.

The Poy family, arriving here as refugees in 1942, was made up of my parents, my brother and myself. Three of us are in this Chamber today. We did not arrive as part of a regular immigration procedure. There was no such thing for a Chinese family at that time in Canadian history...

...I believe that my parents, like so many other immigrants, dreamed their children into being as Canadians... It is customary to talk about how hard immigrants work and how ambitious they are, but those of us who have lived that process, know that it is mainly the dream that counts...

...The dream pulls us on and transforms us into Canadians.

Installation speech, 7 October 1999

伍冰枝

伍冰枝1939年出生于香港，1942年跟着家人以难民身份移居到了加拿大。她在安大略省的渥太华长大，从多伦多大学获得了英文文学硕士学位，然后在法国的苏邦大学从事学术研究。伍冰枝以主播与记者身份开始，在文化艺术和公共服务上有了很大的成就。她在1980年代期间在巴黎被任命为加拿大安大略省驻法国的代表，1992年获颁加拿大联邦的最高荣誉－'加拿大勋章'。1999年，她宣誓就任加拿大总督。

伍氏家族1942年以难民身份来到这里时，包括了我父母、弟弟和我自己。我们其中三个今天在这国会大厅里。我们并不是依照正常的移民手续入境的－对一个华人家庭来说，在加拿大历史里的那时，根本没这回事...

...我相信我父母也像许多其他移民一样，把孩子们梦想成了加拿大人...大家谈起移民们时总是喜欢说他们多么辛苦工作，多有抱负，但我们这些亲身经历过那过程的人，都知道最重要的其实是那梦想...

...是梦想把我们拉向前，把我们变成了加拿大人。

1999年10月7日伍冰枝的宣誓就职演说

yo-yo ma

Yo-Yo Ma was born in Paris in 1955. A world-renowned cellist, he is the winner of the Avery Fisher Prize and numerous other awards. Hailed as 'one of the greatest instrumental talents alive' by Isaac Stern, Ma has performed with orchestras around the world.

马友友

马友友1955年出生于巴黎。这位世界闻名的大提琴家曾荣获极为荣耀的'艾维费雪'奖和其他无数音乐奖项。曾被世界音乐大师艾萨克·史坦赞为'现今最伟大的乐器天才之一'的他，曾经在世界各地和许多交响乐团和乐队合作表演。

maxine hong kingston

Maxine Hong Kingston was born in California in 1940.
A writer of international acclaim, she is known for her
groundbreaking books. In *The Woman Warrior*, Kingston
explored what it was like to grow up as a Chinese-American
girl and in *China Men*, she examined the immigration
experience of Chinese men in America.

Chinese-Americans, when you try to understand what things in you are
Chinese, how do you separate what is peculiar to childhood, to poverty,
insanities, one family, your mother who marked your growing with
stories, from what is Chinese?

Maxine Hong Kingston, *The Woman Warrior*

汤婷婷

汤婷婷1940年出生于加利福尼亚州。她以创史性的书成名，是享誉
国际的作家。她在处女作《女勇士》里讲述了一个美籍华人女孩成
长的故事，而在《金山华人》中探讨了华籍男子移民美国的经历。

美国华裔们，当你尝试了解身上到底哪些部分属于华人，你如何从属于华人的部分，
把仅属于童年、贫穷、疯狂、一家人、讲着故事陪你长大的妈妈，区分开来？

汤婷婷, *The Woman Warrior*

Hollyburn Ridge, Vancouver, British Columbia, Canada, c. 1930

China, c. 1937

hua song

Chinese sojourners and migrants since the mid-nineteenth
century have spawned a bountiful forest of great diversity,
and this writer has flitted from bloom to bloom, well aware
that a single chapter in a book cannot hope to sing the
praise of every trailblazer among the overseas Chinese
community in the world today. *Hua Song*, in praise of the
strength, courage and creativity of this community, invites
all sojourners and migrants to sow good seeds and add to
life's bounty for the generations to come.

华颂

自19世纪中期以来的旅居者和移民构成了一座浓密而丰富多彩的森
林；而本作者只能从这朵花到那朵花四处乱飞，清楚知道仅仅本书
的一个章节绝不可能赞扬海外华人社会里的所有勇士们。《华颂》
颂扬这些海外华人的坚强、勇敢与创造性，请所有旅居者和移民播
下好种子，为来日的后代增添生命丰硕的果实。

澳洲：安身立命

我们是这所学校历史上唯一出现过的亚洲人。和身材高大的澳洲人比起来，我们显得瘦小，像营养不良似的；而刚进学校时我们连一句英语都不会讲。头几个月里，我们面对几乎无休止的骚扰。那些澳洲男孩围住我们，一边跳着一边唱：'清清中国人，他真坏，他真坏'。

那我和我的兄弟们怎么办？我们做了一件英国绅士绝不会做的事－告状首我们向校长告状，他却说他无能为力，因为那些嘲笑我们的人并没有对我们造成身体的伤害，我们只要保护自己就好了。所以我们只好出手反击了。我们以牙还牙、以眼还眼。我们虽然不太会说话，身材也差了对方一截，但我们的愤怒弥补了这些不足。不久之后，这些种族攻击和骚扰减少了。有时，我们很享受这些打斗，完全忘记了我们是因为尊严被冒犯才出手的。

澳洲Wisconsin-Madison大学地质学教授Tuan Yi-Fu回忆起当初刚来到悉尼的时候

华人矿工把澳洲称为'新金山'。但来到这片广阔的土地，尝试发掘机会的人不止有他们。新移民当中还有商人、律师、医生。

我父亲麦世昌1900年代到1930年代之间在墨尔本颇有名气。他是当地最有才华、最伶牙俐齿的律师之一。他1876年出生于维多利亚，是祖父母育有的六个女儿之外唯一的儿子。祖父于1850年代趁着澳洲的淘金热从广东移民过来，淘金热结束后选择定居在Wangaratta。

麦彩蓝

尽管不时发生的反亚暴乱，成千上万个华人已在澳洲成家。达尔文市1966年选出了澳洲历史上第一个华人市长。澳洲华裔，如欧威廉，进入了国会；华裔专业人士，如张任谦医生和1996年的'年度澳洲模范公民'余森美医生等，深受澳洲人民敬重。如今，悉尼、墨尔本、达尔文和坎贝拉的博物馆都设有'澳洲土生华人'展台，以肯定他们对澳洲经济、政治和文化艺术所作出的贡献。

我为我的中华根源感到骄傲，但为自己是澳洲人感到更骄傲。

余森美医生，1996年的'年度澳洲模范公民'

Australia: Fighting for a Place

We were the only Asians—not only then but in the entire history of the school. We were puny, undernourished, compared with the robust Australians, and we didn't, at first, speak a word of English. In the first few months of school, we were subjected to almost relentless harassment. 'Chin chien Chinaman, him very bad', the Australian boys chanted as they danced around us...

So what did my brothers and I do? Well, we did a most un-British thing: we tattled... We then informed our schoolmaster, who simply told us to fend for ourselves, unless the taunters made it physically difficult for us to attend class. And so we fought back, and we gave as good as we got, our righteous fury making up for our deficiencies in swear words and physical size. Soon, the ethnic slurs and harassment started to abate. At times, we enjoyed the fights so much that we quite forgot the offence to dignity that prompted them.

Yi-Fu Tuan, professor emeritus of geography at
the University of Wisconsin-Madison,
recalling his early years in Sydney, Australia

Sin Gum Shan, New Gold Mountain—that was what Chinese goldminers called Australia. But they were not the only ones who came for the opportunities in this great land. Among the newcomers were also merchants, lawyers and doctors.

My father, William Ah Ket rose to prominence in the 1900s–1930s as one of Melbourne's most talented and adroit barristers. He was born in Victoria in 1876, the only son among six daughters of Chinese parents. His father had migrated from Canton [Guangzhou] in the 1850s, and when the Gold Rush in Australia ended, he settled in Wangaratta to raise his family.

Toylaan Ah Ket

Despite occasional anti-Asian sentiment, thousands of Chinese have made Australia their home. In 1966, Darwin elected Australia's first Chinese mayor. Australian-Chinese citizens such as Bill O'Chee serve in parliament, and professionals like Dr Victor Chang and Dr John Yu are honoured. Today, museums in Sydney, Melbourne, Darwin and Canberra celebrate the contributions of Australia-born Chinese in business, government and the arts.

I am proud of my Chinese heritage but even prouder to be an Australian.

Dr John Yu, physician and 1996 Australian of the Year

美国：勇者之梦

我会把自己称为美国华裔。如果非得选其中一个身份，我会说自己是美国人…我只效忠于这个国家，这是我的家。

林璎

林璎1959年出生，成长于美国俄亥俄州雅典城。她父母从中国移民到美国，在俄亥俄州大学教课。父亲是大学艺术学院院长兼陶艺学家，母亲是诗人兼文学教授。林璎21岁时所设计的越战纪念碑方案在全国征选中被选中，她也成了数次攻击的目标。纪念碑于1982年落成，此后每年都吸引了上百万人造访。

林璎所经历的，是成千上万个美籍华人在美国的经历的一部分。新旧华人移民的后代（例如名编剧黄哲伦和'雅虎'创办人之一杨致远）抓住时代的机遇，在各自领域里大展拳脚。美籍华人如今已成为美国社会中重要的部分。1959年，邝友良成为第一个被选入美国国会的美籍华人。自1960年代中期起，新浪潮的华人移民就一直不断地涌入美国。他们的出现，给美国由于本土出生的华人搬走而显得沉寂下来的唐人街注入了新的活力。美籍华人也正努力重新认识并保留他们的文化传统和遗产，随之出现了许多众多的华文报章、出版物、华人的语言学校以及公司机构。

America: Dreams of the Brave

I would identify myself as Chinese American. If I had to choose one thing over the other, I would choose American... I don't have an allegiance to any country but this one; it is my home.

Maya Ying Lin, architect

Maya Ying Lin was born in 1959 and grew up in Athens, Ohio. Her parents taught at Ohio University and had come to America from China. Her father was dean of the art school and a ceramic artist; her mother was a poet and teacher of literature. When Lin was 21, her design for the Vietnam Veterans Memorial was chosen in a national competition, and she was the subject of many attacks. The memorial was dedicated in 1982 and is visited by millions each year.

Maya Lin's journey mirrors that of thousands of modern-day Chinese-Americans, and the descendants of old and new immigrants (like playwright David Henry Hwang and Jerry Yang, the cofounder of Yahoo) are seizing their opportunities and making their mark in their chosen fields. There is a growing Chinese American presence in the country—in politics, Hiram Fong was the first Chinese American to be elected to the US Senate in 1959. Since the mid-1960s, there has been a steady influx of new immigrants, and their presence has revitalised many Chinatowns that were declining as local-born Chinese Americans moved away from them. Numerous Chinese newspapers, publications, schools and businesses have flourished as Chinese Americans seek to rediscover and preserve their heritage.

经历雨打风吹，
他们乘风破浪、穿海越洋，
方亲异乡土。

日出日落、昼来夜去，到白头；
果腹、养息，生儿育女，茹苦抚育，
看着子女结婚生子，香火延续。

互语‘光阴如梭！’
驻足回望，嗟叹惊奇，
一世代已过。

落叶浮萍业已生根，
常作之地亦成家土，‘落地生根’，
人落异土，根已生成。

林苏贞

Washed by the rain and combed by the winds,
  They had ridden the stormy oceans,
    Flown across the heavens
      And kissed the earth of foreign shores.

From sunrise to sunset, from one day to the next,
  Till their hair turned white,
They ate; they slept; they bore children
  And watched them grow,
    Watched them get married
      And in turn bear children of their own.

How time flies, they said to one another.
  Then, gazing down at their feet one day,
    They were surprised.
      A generation had passed.

Roots had grown into the ground
  Of their daily living.
    Luodi shenggen,
      They had fallen to earth and sprouted roots.

Suchen Christine Lim

CHINA

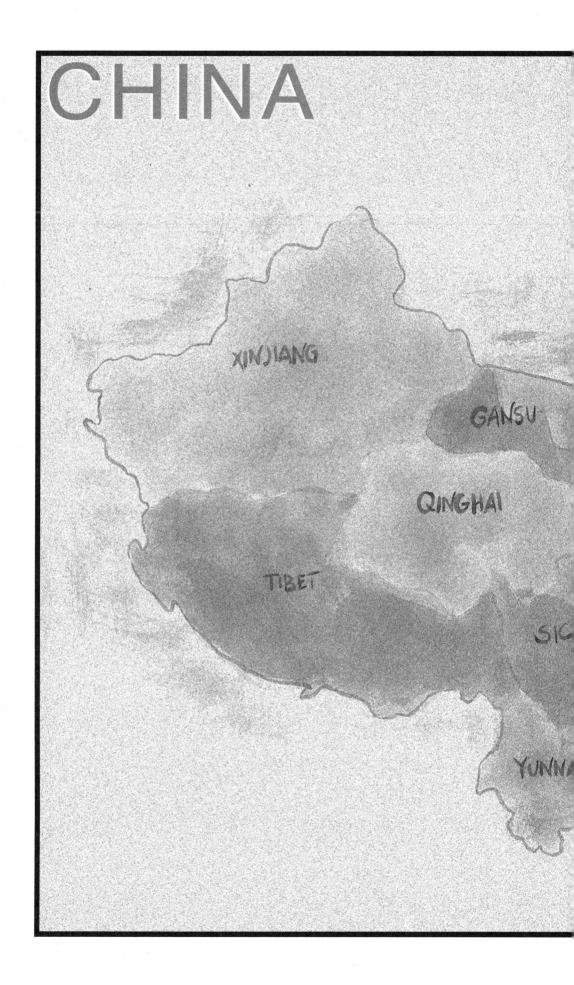

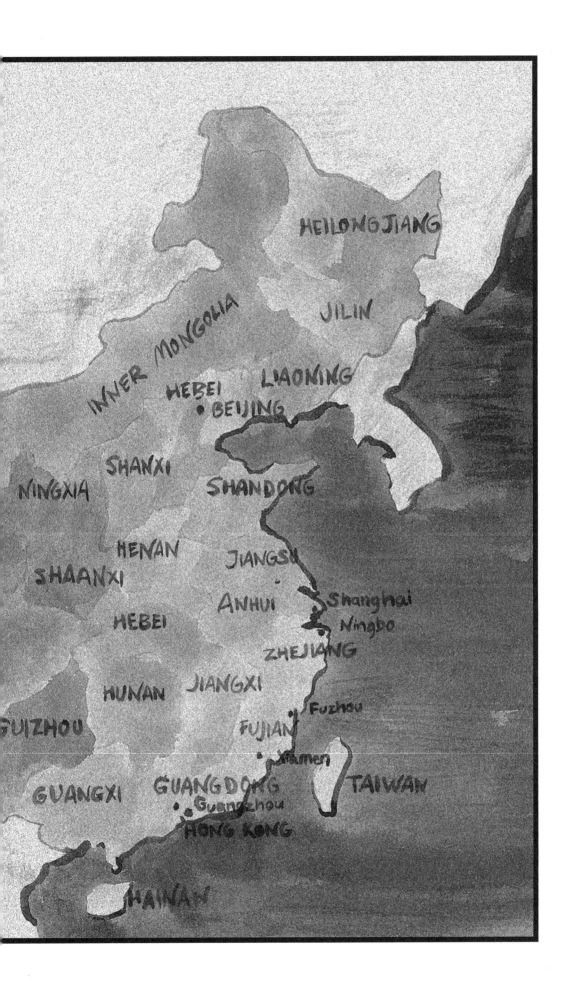

259

text sources

Gold

Pg 19: from *China Men* by Maxine Hong Kingston, Vintage, 1989
Pg 21: Hakka drum song adapted from *Taishan Xinxi Gang* website
Pg 24 (top): from *North of Capricorn: The Untold Story of Australia's North* by Henry Reynolds, Allen & Unwin, Australia, 2003; (bottom): from *Translation of Chinese Folk Rhymes* by Oral History Centre, Singapore, 1994
Pg 26 (top): from *Discussion of Piracy, Vol. I*
Pg 27: from *The Fundamental Laws and a Selection from the Supplementary Statutes of the Penal Code of China* by Sir George Thomas Staunton (trans.), London, 1810
Pg 29 (top): from *The Chinese Abroad* by HF McNair, Commercial Press, Shanghai, 1933; (centre): from *The Cuban Commission Report: The Hidden History of the Chinese in Cuba*, introduction by Denise Helly, Baltimore and London, The Johns Hopkins University Press, 1993; (bottom): from *Report on the Condition of Chinese Labourers in the Colony, paper 22* by the Straits Settlements Legislative Council, Singapore, 1876
Pg 30: from *Opium and Gold: A History of the Chinese Goldminers in New Zealand* by Peter Butler, Alister Taylor, New Zealand, 1977
Pg 33 (top): from *The Chinese American Family Album* by Dorothy and Thomas Hoobler, Oxford University Press, New York, 1994; (bottom): from 'From the Orient Direct' by Albert S Evans, *Atlantic Monthly 24*, 1869; excerpted in *The Chinese American Family Album* by Dorothy and Thomas Hoobler, Oxford University Press, New York, 1994
Pg 39 (top): from *The Bathurst Free Press*, 26 May and 1 September 1858; excerpted in *The Great White Walls are Built: Immigration to North America and Australasia 1836-1888* by Charles A Price, the Australian Institute of International Affairs with Australian University National Press, 1974; (centre): from *The Cuban Commission Report: The Hidden History of the Chinese in Cuba*, introduction by Denise Helly, Baltimore and London, The Johns Hopkins University Press, 1993; (bottom): from *Chinese Coolie Emigration to Countries within the British Empire* by Persia Crawford Campbell, Frank Cass & Co Ltd, London, 1971

Vietnam

Pg 41: from *The Encyclopedia of the Chinese Overseas* by Lynn Pan (ed.), Archipelago Press and Landmark Books, Singapore, 1998

Pioneers

Pg 47: from *Songs of Gold Mountain: Cantonese Rhymes from San Francisco Chinatown* by Marlon K Hom, University of California Press, Berkeley, 1987
Pg 49: from *The Chinese in America: A Narrative History* by Iris Chang, Viking, New York, 2003
Pg 53 (top): from *The Tuapeka Times*, 10 September 1884, excerpted in *Windows on a Chinese Past: How the Cantonese Goldseekers and Their Heirs Settled in New Zealand, Vol. I* by James Ng, Otago Heritage Books, Dunedin, 1993; (second from top): from *Symons Report on the Upper Columbia River and the Great Plain of Columbia* by TW Symons, Ye Galleon Press, Washington, 1882, excerpted in *Chinese Gold Miners of the Mid Columbia Region* by JJ Sharpe, the US Department of Energy, Richland Operations Office, 1999; (second from bottom): from *The Chinese in America: A Narrative History* by Iris Chang, Viking, New York, 2003; (bottom): from *British Malaya* by Frank A Swettenham, London, 1948
Pg 65 (top): from *The Border Morning Herald*, 13 August 1945, excerpted in *The New Gold Mountain* by CF Yong, Raphael Arts Pty Ltd, South Australia, 1977; (centre): From *The Chinese Australian Herald*, 15 June 1907, excerpted in *The New Gold Mountain* by CF Yong, Raphael Arts Pty Ltd, South Australia, 1977
Pg 65 (second from bottom): from 'The Chinese in California' by Henryk Sienkiewicz, *California Historical Society Quarterly 34*,1955, excerpted in *The Chinese American Family Album* by Dorothy and Thomas Hoobler, Oxford University Press, New York, 1994; (bottom): from *North of Capricorn: The Untold Story of Australia's North* by Henry Reynolds, Allen & Unwin, Australia, 2003
Pg 72: from *The Chinese in the New Territory* (revised edition) by Timothy G Jones, Northern Territory University Press, Darwin, 1997
Pg 75 (centre): from *The Chinese American Family Album* by Dorothy and Thomas Hoobler, Oxford University Press, New York, 1994; (bottom): from *The Chinese in America: A Narrative History* by Iris Chang, Viking, New York, 2003
Pg 81 (top): from *Sojourners and Settlers: Chinese Migrants in Hawaii* by Clarence E Glick, Hawaii Chinese History Centre and the University Press of Hawaii, Hawaii, 1980

The Caribbean and South America: Scattered Seeds

Pg 85 (top): from *The Cuban Commission Report: The Hidden History of the Chinese in Cuba*, introduction by Denise Helly, Baltimore and London, The Johns Hopkins University Press, 1993

Chinatown

Pg 93 (top): from *The Chinese in Southeast Asia* (second edition) by Victor Purcell, Oxford University Press, London, 1965; (centre): from *Our New Possession* by James Lyng, Melbourne Publishing Co, Melbourne, 1919; (bottom): from 'Singapore versus Kuala Lumpur' by Margaret Wilson, 1934, excerpted in *Traveller's Singapore* by John Bastin, Oxford University Press, Singapore, 1994
Pg 101 (top): from *The Chinese American Family Album* by Dorothy and Thomas Hoobler, Oxford University Press, New York, 1994; (bottom): from *The Savage Australia* by Knut Dahl, Philip Adam, London, 1926, excerpted in *North of Capricorn: The Untold Story of Australia's North* by Henry Reynolds, Allen & Unwin, Australia, 2003
Pg 105 (top): from *Ancestors: Chinese in Colonial Australia* by Jan Ryan, Fremantle Arts Centre Press, Australia, 1995; (bottom): from *Singapore Patrol* by Alec Dixon, London, 1935, excerpted in *Rickshaw Coolie: A People's History of Singapore (1880–1940)* by James Francis Warren, Oxford University Press, Singapore, 2003
Pg 106 (top): from *Strangers from a Different Shore: A History of Asian Americans* (revised edition) by Ronald Takaki, Back Bay Books, New York, 1998; (bottom): from *The Chinese in America: A Narrative History* by Iris Chang, Viking, New York, 2003
Pg 109: from *Songs of Gold Mountain: Cantonese Rhymes from San Francisco Chinatown* by Marlon K Hom, University of California Press, Berkeley, 1987
Pg 111 (centre): from 'Chinatowns: A Study in Symbiosis and Assimilation' by Ching Chao Wu, University of Chicago Press, Chicago, 1928, excerpted in *Sojourners and Settlers: Chinese Migrants in Hawaii* by Clarence E Glick, Hawaii Chinese History Centre and the University Press of Hawaii, Hawaii, 1980; (bottom): from *Sojourners and Settlers: Chinese Migrants in Hawaii* by Clarence E Glick, Hawaii Chinese History Centre and the University Press of Hawaii, Hawaii, 1980

Women

Pg 127 (top): from *Chinatown: An Album of a Singapore Community* Times Books and Oral History Department, Singapore, 1983, excerpted in *Ah Ku and Karayuki-san: Prostitution in Singapore 1870–1940* by Warren James Francis, Oxford University Press, Singapore, 1993
Pg 131: from *Songs of Gold Mountain: Cantonese Rhymes from San Francisco Chinatown* by Marlon K Hom, University of California Press, Berkeley, 1987
Pg 132 (top): from *The Chinese American Family Album* by Dorothy and Thomas Hoobler, Oxford University Press, New York, 1994
Pg 135: from *Superior Servants: Legendary Cantonese Amahs of the Far East* by Kenneth Gaw, Oxford University Press, Singapore, 1988
Pg 139 (centre): from *Superior Servants: Legendary Cantonese Amahs of the Far East* by Kenneth Gaw, Oxford University Press, Singapore, 1988; (bottom): from *Superior Servants: Legendary Cantonese Amahs of the Far East* by Kenneth Gaw, Oxford University Press, Singapore, 1988
Pg 143 (top): from *Strong as Mountains, Free as Water: The Samsui Women* website by Cheryl Sim; (second from top): from *Strong as Mountains, Free as Water: The Samsui Women* website by Cheryl Sim; (third from top): from *Strong as Mountains, Free as Water: The Samsui Women* website by Cheryl Sim; (fourth from top): from *The Chinese in America: A Narrative History* by Iris Chang, Viking, New York, 2003; (bottom): from *The Chinese in America: A Narrative History* by Iris Chang, Viking, New York, 2003
Pg 146 (bottom): from *The Ethnic Chinese in East and Southeast Asia* by Yen Ching-Hwang, Times Academic Press, Singapore, 2002
Pg 147 (bottom): from *Unbound Feet: A Social History of Chinese Women in San Francisco* by Judy Yung, University of California Press, Berkeley, 1995
Pg 150: from *Home Away from Home: Life Stories of Chinese Women in New Zealand* by Ip Manying, New Women's Press, Auckland, 1990

Singapore

Pg 153 (bottom): from *No Other City: An Ethos Anthology of Urban Poetry* by Ethos Books, Singapore, 2000

New Zealand

Pg 155 (centre): from *A Place to Stand: The Chun Family Experience* by Kirsten Wong, excerpted in *Unfolding History, Evolving Identity: The Chinese in New Zealand* by Ip Manying, Auckland University Press, New Zealand, 2003

Bonds

Pg 159 (top): from *Strangers from a Different Shore: A History of Asian Americans* (revised edition) by Ronald Takaki, Back Bay Books, New York, 1998; (bottom): from *Sojourners and Settlers: Chinese Migrants in Hawaii* by Clarence E Glick, Hawaii Chinese History Centre and the University Press of Hawaii, Hawaii, 1980
Pg 164 (centre): from *The Encyclopedia of the Chinese Overseas* by Lynn Pan (ed.), Archipelago Press and Landmark Books, Singapore, 1998

image sources

Pg 165 (top): from *The Encyclopedia of the Chinese Overseas* by Lynn Pan (ed.), Archipelago Press and Landmark Books, Singapore, 1998

Pg 169 (centre): from *Colour, Confusion and Concessions: The History of the Chinese in South Africa* by Melanie Yap and Dianne Leong Man, Hong Kong University Press, Hong Kong, 1996

Pg 171 (centre): from *Sojourners and Settlers: Chinese Migrants in Hawaii* by Clarence E Glick, Hawaii Chinese History Centre and the University Press of Hawaii, Hawaii, 1980

Pg 173 (bottom): from *The Chinese in America: A Narrative History* by Iris Chang, Viking, New York, 2003

Pg 175 (top): from *Strangers from a Different Shore: A History of Asian Americans* (revised edition) by Ronald Takaki, Back Bay Books, New York, 1998; (centre): from *Strangers from a Different Shore: A History of Asian Americans* (revised edition) by Ronald Takaki, Back Bay Books, New York, 1998; (bottom): from *Pages from Yesteryear: A Look at the Printed Works of Singapore, 1819–1959* by Lee Geok Boi, the Singapore Heritage Society, Singapore, 1989

Malaysia

Pg 183 (top): from *A Thousand Miles on an Elephant in the Shan States* by Holt S Hallet, Wm Blackwood & Sons, London, 1890; (bottom): from *The Encyclopedia of the Chinese Overseas* by Lynn Pan (ed.), Archipelago Press and Landmark Books, Singapore, 1998

Food

Pg 191 (bottom): from *Sojourners and Settlers: Chinese Migrants in Hawaii* by Clarence E Glick, Hawaii Chinese History Centre and the University Press of Hawaii, Hawaii, 1980

Pg 197 (top): from *The Importance of Living* by Lin Yutang, Cultured Lotus, Singapore, 1937

India

Pg 203 (centre): from *The Encyclopedia of the Chinese Overseas* by Lynn Pan (ed.), Archipelago Press and Landmark Books, Singapore, 1998

Canada

Pg 205 (top): from *The Concubine's Children* by Denise Chong, Viking, New York, 1994; (second from top): from *The Asian Canadian* website

Rituals

Pg 209: from *Sojourners and Settlers: Chinese Migrants in Hawaii* by Clarence E Glick, Hawaii Chinese History Centre and the University Press of Hawaii, Hawaii, 1980

Pg 211 (top): from *Fistful of Colours* by Suchen Christine Lim, SNP Editions, Singapore, 2003; (bottom): from *The Life of Quong Tart: How a Foreigner Succeeded in a British Community* by Margaret Tart, Ben Franklin Printing Works, Sydney, 1911

Pg 214 (top): from *Sojourners and Settlers: Chinese Migrants in Hawaii* by Clarence E Glick, Hawaii Chinese History Centre and the University Press of Hawaii, Hawaii, 1980

Pg 219 (centre): from *The Chinese in America: A Narrative History* by Iris Chang, Viking, New York, 2003

Pg 222 (bottom): from *The Babas* by Felix Chia, Times Books International, Singapore, 1980

Europe

Pg 225 (top): from *China Awakened* by Tuk Min-Chien TZ, Macmillan, New York, 1922; (centre): from *Chinese in Russia: An Historical Perspective* by Alexander G Larin, from *The Chinese in Europe* by Gregor Benton and Frank N Pieke, Macmillan Press Ltd, London, 1998

Pg 226 (top): from *British Born Chinese* website

Trailblazers

Pg 233: from *Chinese Leadership and Power in Colonial Singapore* by CF Yong, Times Academic Press, Singapore, 1991

Pg 237 (centre): from *The Chinese in America: A Narrative History* by Iris Chang, Viking, New York, 2003

Pg 239: from *Legend from a Jar* by Sylvia Toh Paik Choo, Haw Par Brothers International, Singapore, 1994

Pg 241 (bottom): from *Lee Kuan Yew: The Man and His Ideas* by Han Fook Kwang, Warren Fernandez and Sumiko Tan, Times Editions, Singapore, 1997

Pg 249 (bottom): from *The Woman Warrior* by Maxine Hong Kingston, Vintage, New York, 2000

Australia

Pg 253 (top): from *Who Am I? By* Tuan Yi-Fu, the University of Wisconsin Press, Wisconsin, 1999; (centre): from the *Chinese Heritage of Australian Federation Project* website; (bottom): from *Australian of the Year* website

From *A Vision of the Past: A History of the Early Photography in Singapore* by John Falconer, Times Editions pg 134; Antiques of the Orient, Singapore pg 60; Asian Studies Association of Australia pg 193; from *Asian-Americans in the Old West* by Gail Sakurai, Children's Press pgs 65, 94 (top), 211; Bangkok Bank, Singapore pg 242; the Bancroft Library, University of California, Berkeley pgs 111 (bottom), 189 (bottom); California Historical Society pgs 80, 92, 97, 98, 99, 106, 110, 113, 130, 186; California History Room, California State Library, Sacramento, California pgs 54–55, 74 (bottom); Canadian High Commission, Singapore pgs 246, 247; from *Chinatown: An Album of Singapore* Times Books International pgs 114 (bottom), 115; from *The Chinese Century* by Jonathan Spence and Annping Chin, Random House pg 249; from *Chinese Women in America: A Pictorial History* by Judy Yung, University of Washington Press pgs 108, 149, 146–147; from *The Chinese American Family Album* by Dorothy and Thomas Hoobler, Oxford University Press pg 189 (top); from *Chinois de France: Un Siecle de Presences de 1900 a Nos Jours* by Live Yu-sion, Editions Memoire Collective pg 201; from *Cina a Milano* by Renato Minetto, AIM pgs 114 (top), 116, 177 (bottom); from *Colour, Confusion and Concessions: The Story of the Chinese in South Africa* by Melanie Yap and Dianne Leong Man, Hong Kong University Press pgs 22 (top), 56 (bottom left), 76–77, 168; Connecticut Historical Society pgs 169, 236; from *Conversations with IM Pei: Light is the Key* by Gero von Boehm and IM Pei, Prestel Publishing pgs 244, 245; William Patrick Cranley pgs 178, 218 (top), 223 (top); from *The Diggers of China: The Story of Chinese on the Goldfields* by Jean Gittins, Quartet Books pg 73; from *Dragons on the Long White Cloud: The Making of Chinese New Zealanders* by Manying Ip, Tandem Press pgs 177 (bottom), 179 (top); from *Encounters with China: Merchants, Missionaries and Mandarins* by Trea Wiltshire, FormAsia pgs 24–25, 104 (bottom); Foreign and Commonwealth Office Library, London pgs 36–37; from *From the Family Album: Portraits from the Lee Brothers Studio, Singapore 1910–1925* National Heritage Board, Singapore pgs 160–161; from *Georgette Chen* by Jane Chia, Singapore History Museum pg 143; Getty Images pg 8; Robert Glick, Chinatown Historical Museum, New York pg 173 (top); The Golden Threads Project pgs 53, 145, 171, 214 (left); from *Gum San: Land of the Gold Mountain* by the High Desert Museum pgs 59 (bottom), 81 (bottom), 94 (bottom), 102, 103 (bottom), 148, 159, 162, 166, 192, 198 (top), 208, 217 (bottom), 250, 251; *Harper's Magazine* pgs 28, 29; Hawaii State Archives pgs 23, 62; from *History of the Chinese Clan Associations in Singapore* by National Archives of Singapore pgs 20, 31; from *Home Away from Home: Life Stories of Chinese Women in New Zealand* by Manying Ip, New Women's Press pgs 150, 151 (bottom), 151 (top), 199; Idaho State Historical Society pg 132; Imperial War Museum, London pgs 58, 63 (top), 63 (bottom); Geoffrey Jeffreys pg 66 (top); Johns Hopkins University Press pg 33; Betty Woon Jung, from *Chinese-American Portraits: Personal Histories 1828–1988* by Ruthanne Lum McCann, University of Washington Press pg 218 (bottom); Koninkklijk Instituut voor Taal-, Land- en Volkenkunde, Leiden pgs 5, 35, 50 (top), 50 (bottom), 51, 59 (top), 79, 82, 83 (top), 83 (bottom), 93, 176, 198 (bottom), 212–213, 216, 220–221; from *Masters* pg 264; Mary Kathryn Green McCarthy, from *Chinese-American Portraits: Personal Histories 1828–1988* by Ruthanne Lum McCann, University of Washington Press pg 234; Scott Merrillees pg 223 (bottom); Mitchell Library, State Library of New South Wales pgs 210, 214 (right); National Archives and Records Administration, USA pgs 32, 38, 39; National Archives of Malaysia pg 46; National Archives of Singapore pgs 12, 26–27, 61, 70–71, 95 (bottom), 96, 100, 104 (top), 105, 112, 140, 141, 142, 158, 163, 164, 165, 170, 187, 190, 191, 196, 197, 200, 219, 222 (top), 230, 240; National Library of Australia pgs 52, 72 (top), 95 (top); Oakland Museum of California pg 111 (top); Office of Multicultural Affairs, Australia pg 48; from *On Gold Mountain: The 10-Year Odyssey of a Chinese-American Family* by Lisa See, St Martin's Press pgs 101, 217 (top); from *Pages from Yesteryear: A Look at the Printed Works of Singapore, 1819–1959* by Lee Geok Boi, Singapore Heritage Society pgs 172, 175 (top), 175 (bottom); from *Picturing Chinatown: Art and Orientalism in San Francisco* by Anthony W Lee, University of California Press pgs 90–91, 173 (bottom), 174, 188; Pontifical Institute of Foreign Missions, Milan, Leoni Nani Collection pg 19; Provincial Archives of British Columbia pg 34 (bottom); Public Records Office, Government Records Service, Hong Kong pgs 16–17; from the Presbyterian Church of Aotearoa New Zealand, photograph by Reverend Alexander Don pg 57; Shanghai Historical Museum pg 18; Southern Pacific Railroad pg 74 (top); State Library of New South Wales pg 103 (top); from *Superior Servants: The Legendary Cantonese Amahs of the Far East* by Kenneth Gaw, Oxford University Press pgs 129, 135, 136, 138, 139; from *Taming the Coolie Beast* by Jan Breman, Oxford University Press, New Delhi pgs 1, 34 (top), 49, 66 (bottom), 69; Eleanor Wong Telemaque, from *Chinese-American Portraits: Personal Histories 1828–1988* by Ruthanne Lum McCann, University of Washington Press pg 6; from *This Bitter Sweet Soil: The Chinese in California Agriculture, 1860–1910* by Sucheng Chan, University of California Press pgs 64, 68; University of Hawaii Press pgs 133, 179 (bottom); from *Unsubmissive Women: Chinese Prostitutes in Nineteenth-Century San Francisco* by Benson Tong, University of Oklahoma Press pgs 124, 126, 127; Vancouver Public Library pg 78; from *Windows on a Chinese Past* by James Ng, Otago Heritage Books pgs 56 (top), 56 (bottom right), 67 (top), 67 (bottom), 256; YMCA of America Archives pgs 22 (bottom), 72 (bottom).

Every effort has been made to trace copyright holders, and the publishers would like to apologise to anyone who has not been formally acknowledged.

resources index